Practical
Transactional
Analysis
in Management

Practical Transactional Analysis in Management

JAMES H. MORRISON
Lawrence-Leiter & Company

JOHN J. O'HEARNE
O'Hearne Medical Corporation

ADDISON-WESLEY PUBLISHING COMPANY

Reading, Massachusetts • Menlo Park, California • London
Amsterdam • Don Mills, Ontario • Sydney

ISBN 0-201-04898-1
ABCDEFGHIJ-DO-7987

Preface

One of management's biggest responsibilities is to increase the efficiency of workers. If employees are dissatisfied with each other or with the place where they work, their efficiency is likely to be substandard. Organizations suffer huge losses of human effectiveness as a result of the negative feelings of those who work there. Such feelings as doubt and indecision, embarrassment, fear, and anger drain energy from both the individual and the organization, and may result in psychological games or industrial sabotage that exact a heavy toll in time and money.

We believe that managers can prevent many such feelings and help remedy others. We do *not* believe that managers should be psychotherapists who spend most of their time trying to cure people's bad feelings. However, managers can learn skills to facilitate working with people and getting them to work together with greater efficiency and greater ease than is found in many organizations.

In our sixty-six combined years of experience in working professionally with people, we have found TA (Transactional

Analysis) to be the simplest tool now available for such purposes. Our intent in this book is to make TA operational, for we believe that it can be understood and used without resorting to either "cute" language or complicated psychological concepts. Our objective has been to write a book that can be used either independently by the individual manager in his or her own self-development plan, or as a guide within a structured training program.

To help achieve these aims, we have included suggested activities at the end of many of the chapters. Simply reading this book will help you understand how to reach some of the TA goals. Studying it will help you reach even more. And reading, studying, and completing the suggested activities will not only help you understand our methods, but will also show you how we use TA on the job. If you do study and complete the activities, we believe you will share our belief that TA is today's simplest, most efficient method for understanding and modifying human behavior.

Kansas City, Missouri   JHM
November 1976   JJO

Contents

Contents

x
Contents

1

Introduction

Although this is a book primarily for managers, the basic human interactions it deals with are equally applicable to off-the-job situations—at home, with family or friends, or at work in volunteer community organizations. Transactional Analysis (TA), an approach to understanding and improving the human interactions crucial to good management in all aspects of organizational and family life, provides the framework for our discussion. The concept was originally developed by Dr. Eric Berne, a California psychiatrist. In 1958, Dr. Berne founded a small society to study its use; by 1976, this group had expanded to 10,000 members and TA had become a familiar term to many Americans.

Six common English words, all given special meaning, comprise the basic language of TA. One of its greatest appeals is that it avoids traditional psychological jargon. The advantages of TA for managers are:

1. The basics are simple to learn.

2. It is readily demonstrable.

3. It provides a means of reducing the amount of bad feelings experienced by an individual.

4. It increases the efficient use of time.

5. It can be used to improve the efficiency of communications.

6. It is as applicable at home as it is at work.

7. It reinforces and complements other management-development activities, including training in communications, leadership, brainstorming, management by objectives, job enrichment, and other similar programs.

The disadvantages of TA are:

1. Few scientific studies of outcomes are available.

2. Ego states, basic to understanding and utilizing TA, are difficult to define (although easy to teach and demonstrate operationally).

3. If inappropriately applied, TA tends to encourage "amateur psychologizing."

4. The proliferation of new theories and extensions of old ones outpace the scientific evidence to support them.

5. TA jargon may lead to more "cuteness" than insight into human encounter.

6. It can be used as a put-down, or a discount, in interpersonal relations.

At present writing, there seems to be no limit to the usefulness of TA in business, industry, and government, or to the levels within the organization where it can be profitably utilized. Training programs for employees, especially for individuals in contact with the public or the customer, have multiplied over the past ten years. Meter readers, government clerks conducting business with citizens, bank tellers, stewardesses, and salespersons are only a few of the job titles for which specific TA training programs have been developed.

Managerial and supervisory skills training has frequently been designed to include transactional analysis, primarily as a communication-improvement technique. However, one of the major problems encountered is the reluctance of top management to submit to the discipline of continuing management education by participating in the TA training. This results in an inability on the part of top management to discuss intelligently the basic concepts of transactional analysis with other managers, much less practice them.

One of the more recent developments is the incorporation of TA into organizational and teamwork development activities. This has provided a welcome relief from earlier, sometimes disastrous, sensitivity training, which has been used in the past as a teamwork improvement method. Transactional analysis seems to provide the authenticity of a growth-oriented process that appeals as much to an individual's sense of personal growth ("It's good for me as a person") as to the individual's occupational skills ("It's good for the organization, too"). These two factors have become increasingly crucial to the acceptance and successful application of concepts conveyed by management training-and-development activities. Transactional analysis supplies both.

A number of books present accurately, and in detail, the technical aspect of transactional analysis. Some of these are listed in the bibliography following Chapter 8. However, this book is designed to provide for managers a self-contained explanation of the practical aspects of transactional analysis. Technical footnotes, extensive exercises, and detailed references to the origin of each key TA thought have been abandoned in favor of presenting easy-to-read, easy-to-assimilate, and easy-to-apply concepts that deal with the everyday tasks of managers and supervisors. The jargon of some TA programs and publications has been eliminated insofar as humanly possible —hopefully, without sacrificing the authentic fun that TA holds for people of all ages and backgrounds.

The results of TA training in industry have been reported in various technical journals. Case histories have been presented in elaborate detail in a collection edited by Dorothy Jongeward(11)*. As more rigorous before-and-after measures are included in program designs, we can look forward to even more-effective programs in the future.

In the end analysis, this is a book about management—concept and practice. Transactional analysis has been applied in four ways:

1. In many instances, TA offers fresh, deep insights into the functioning of a manager's interpersonal skills. The significance of strokes, for example, provides an *explanation* of the urgency and primacy of a basic human need. It also explains some otherwise puzzling behaviors.

2. TA frequently supplies a *process* for implementing well-established management and motivation theories. For example, much of the motivational management literature deals with the need to supply "motivators," or to use a "Theory Y" approach, in managing people (see Chapter 6).

---

*The authors were consultants on a passenger-relations improvement project for a large international airline which is described in that publication, p. 125 (see "References" for complete reference). Our conviction is that training programs in TA need careful tailoring and design if tangible results are to be achieved.

The question asked by most managers is: "How do I do this?" This book supplies some operations gleaned from TA to facilitate use of the theory on the job.

3. TA contributes to *better insight* into some of the practices of effective managers which have been developed by trial and error over a period of many years. For example, the utilization of effective "praise" and constructive "criticism" has evolved over years of management practice. TA clarifies why some praise and criticism is positive and some is negative.

4. When things go better at home, they usually go better at work also. TA, as a personal-growth vehicle, will help managers *be more effective* on the job as they attain greater competence in interpersonal relationships off the job.

By using TA, you can study and change your bad feelings or inefficient functioning in dealing with others. At the same time, you can also help others—associates, customers, subordinates, family, friends—feel and function better.

Shall we begin?

2

Who's Doing the Talking?

Transactional analysis is the simplest way we know to understand and modify, if necessary, human behavior. It is the study of moves people make in their dealings with each other and is based on the idea that people's interactions resemble moves in a game. People making such moves are sometimes perfectly clear about their purposes and can predict the results of their moves. For example, if a manager insults an employee, the manager can predict how that employee will feel and react. TA also teaches how people make moves, or transactions, of which they are not aware. For instance, a manager reviewing a performance appraisal with an employee may speak words that would sound merely descriptive if printed on a page and read aloud. However, if these same words are spoken in a highly critical tone of voice, the employee may listen more to the voice tone than to the words. He may be reminded of an old proverb: "What you are speaks so loudly that I cannot hear what you say." TA helps us to be aware of the moves we make in our daily transactions with others and to predict the consequences of such moves; it then teaches us how to make such transactions more efficient and, often, much more pleasant.

DEVELOPMENT OF EGO STATES

Let's see how it works. And, since human beings are complex, at least part of the time, let's start with the simplest model we can find, a newborn infant. Babies generally feel either good or bad and don't hesitate to let their feelings clearly show. When they feel bad, they may fuss, cry, and kick. If they are fortunate, someone responds to their need and helps them feel good again. They are picked up, changed if necessary, their skin is stroked, they may be rocked or hear a song, or someone may divert them by playing with them. Before long, this infant finds comfort by putting a thumb into the mouth or attracts attention by crying to relieve discomforts. The child is actually learning to predict what will happen when it behaves in certain ways. As the child matures and moves around on its own, it meets some limits. Parents now say "no-no" to it at times. The child is stopped from hurting itself on hot stoves, sharp objects, or out in the street. Eventually, children learn the "no-no's." Especially if they are watched, they are likely to say no-no to themselves. They may even slap their own hands as they do so. At even this young stage, children are beginning to record in their own minds the directions and commands—the do's and don't's—of parents and other caretakers. With further maturation, children look for facts, calculate odds, and make their own decisions instead of accepting what their parents taught them. All parents face the dilemma of deciding when their child is capable of making decisions without parental assistance.

In reviewing these stages of development, we now have the basis for what transactional analysis calls *ego states*. The originator of this term, Dr. Eric Berne, defined an ego state as "a system of feelings accompanied by a related set of behavior patterns." More simply, "ego states" refers to the chief ways that individuals demonstrate their states of being in the world. The infant who responded all over when feeling good or bad is entirely Child. So is Joe at a football game when he jumps up and down and yells with excitement. When one can predict the consequences of one's own behavior, one has developed an Adult ego state. When Mary wants to tell her boss that he is fouling up her filing system, she uses her Adult and predicts what will happen if she lets him know how angry she is. She may then decide on a more effective way to get him to stay out of the files.

When people remember their parents' no-no's, they are developing tape recordings of what their actual parents were like—that is, they are developing a Parent ego state. This ego state may be seen, for example, when you consider calling in to say you are sick on the day before a three-day weekend off from work. Your Parent ego state will tell you, "That's not right." On another occasion, you may consider firing an employee. While your first impulse is to get it over with quickly, your Parent might say, "It's not right to kick that person out without a warning, without seeing what we can do to help."

These ego states are acquired long before reaching adulthood or becoming an actual parent of one's own child. Consequently, when writing about ego states, we capitalize the terms Parent, Adult, and Child to differentiate them from parents, adults, and children. All three ego states are found in each individual and, although only one ego state at a time has power to act, the other two states may be observing. As an illustration, consider your response when told a joke. You hear the words in your Adult, then get the point of the joke and laugh from your Child ego state.

Since the individual can "come on" from each of these states separately, we represent them with three superimposed circles as shown in Fig. 1. By the time big brother is six years old, he may use his Parent ego state, copied from his parents, to yell at a younger sister, "Don't go in the street!" He may then give her information from his Adult ego state that the drivers of cars might not see her and might run into her. When he is in his Child ego state, he himself may forget and chase a ball into the street.

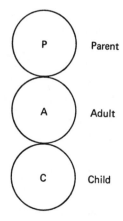

Fig. 1 The ego state circles

To demonstrate how adult individuals shift from one ego state to another, consider an instance in which a manager is reviewing performance with an employee, Joe. If Joe responds with anger, yells, and pounds the table, you would probably say that he is acting like a child. In TA terms, we say that Joe is in his Child ego state. In this state, he feels, thinks, acts, and talks like a child no older than eight years of age. He is not imitating a child; he is not playing the role of a child. At that moment, for all practical purposes, Joe *is* a Child—the same child he was when very young.

The employee's explosion may actually have been triggered by the manager. If the manager sounded critical or sarcastic, didn't recognize any of the employee's good points, and shook an index finger in Joe's face during their meeting, the manager would have been in a Parent ego state. The Child ego state in Joe responded as if he were being criticized by one of his own parents.

Are all Parent ego states critical? No more than are all actual parents critical. When children are small, their actual parents serve two primary purposes: (1) to nurture, nourish, comfort, sustain, and stroke their children so that the children feel good a reasonable amount of time; and (2) to set limits on their children's behavior so they don't hurt themselves. As the children grow older, the parents teach them, sometimes with critical tones and expressions, what they must do to get along in their particular part of the world.

On this functional basis we divide the primary Parent ego state into substates: Nurturing Parent and Critical Parent. This subdivision of the Parent ego state is represented in Fig. 2.

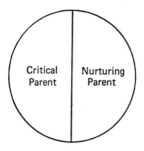

Fig. 2 Subdivision of Parent ego state

A very important feature in TA is the belief that the Parent ego state is recorded deep in our brain and that such recordings are made when we are quite young. Think back for a moment to a direction your parents gave you when you were very small. One that many of us heard is, "Eat everything on your plate. Don't you know there are children starving on the other side of the world?" We know one airline stewardess who began to gain weight while working for the airline. On a visit home, she blamed her mother for this, saying, "You always told us to eat everything on our plate." The other children in the family said this was not so. Then she remembered that while her family had been on an airplane trip to a foreign country, her mother had told her to eat everything on her plate while she was traveling so that she would not be hungry before they got to the next restaurant. This stewardess had been acting like a good little girl, listening to her mother tell her to clean her plate while traveling. This is a sample of the way we all replay those "videotape recordings" of our parents and other early teachers. When she looked with her Adult at what she had been doing, she made plans to keep some food with her when traveling across many time zones to avoid over-eating. Within six weeks she was down to her normal weight.

This example underscores the importance of looking at facts through today's eyes, not through those of our Child or Parent, both of whom were recorded early and are often out of date. To begin a new job may be frightening, especially to the Child ego state. On the job, the Adult facts are there to be learned if you want to do well in the new job. The Parent in you may feel like saying, "That's not the way to do it," when you are shown a new process. Your Adult will tell you that this will not be a wise move in your very first day on the new job.

The Adult ego state is a data processor, almost devoid of feelings.* If decisions are made entirely by the Adult, they will be based on factual information, not based on strong feelings. Since the core of our tape-recorded Parent is primarily our picture of what our own parents were like, decisions made from here will be strongly connected with nurturing and setting limits and with criticism. In our Parent ego state, we are not entirely what our own parents were, for we may record new data and change attitudes and opinions. For example, most parents learn enough with their first child that they treat the second child differently, becoming different kinds of parents than they were the first time. You may also update your Parent by books such as this one, by management-training courses, supervision, etc. Here you learn new ways to treat yourself and others.

Let's take another look at the Child ego state. Children in every society in the world do what they feel like until they learn that they must adjust to the world around them. This represents the first step children experience in adjusting to situations they will encounter as adults. They must adjust to schools, teams, businesses, small groups, and large groups. How does the child do this? He or she uses the developing Adult to predict consequences and regulate behavior. The child does not stop playing, grabbing, hitting, teasing, crying, laughing and the like. Those remain functions of the Natural Child ego state, a subdivision of the Child.

That part of the Child ego state which adapts to what the youngster knows must be done to please another in order to "get along" is called the Adapted Child response. If you think

---

*We believe the only "feeling" in the Adult is the satisfying feeling of acquiring a new skill—the "I really did it!" moment. In motivation theory this may be identified with "intrinsic" motivation, close to the Achievement motivation of McClelland or the Learning and Growth motivator of Herzberg.

of the Adapted Child as looking over his shoulder to check for the approval of his parents, then you will understand the Adapted Child. The little girl who picks up the baby and imitates her mother as she holds the baby is not only learning how to hold babies. She is also adapting to what people want her to do. She will be rewarded with smiles and perhaps with comments such as, "Isn't she a sweet little mother?" If she later has a baby of her own, she may mother the child either from her Parent ego state or from her Adapted Child. If from the latter, she will be extremely sensitive to others' opinions of how she should rear her child, since she will be looking for approval as she did when she herself was small. If she mothers from her Parent ego state, she will care primarily about the welfare of her baby, not whether others approve or not. Similarly, if a little boy learns that he gets the most attention when he breaks things around the house, he may adapt by getting lots of negative attention. Later, on the job, he may specialize in similarly breaking things, creating safety hazards for himself and others, if he is in his Adapted Child ego state instead of

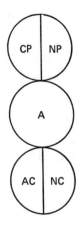

Fig. 3   Ego states with subdivisions

his Adult. We represent the subdivisions of the Child by splitting the Child into Adapted and Natural Child. Now, our picture of the entire person with important subdivisions looks like Fig. 3.

We are stressing ego states because they are the bare bones on which hang all the other concepts contained in this book. If you understand them, you can understand Transactional Analysis. When you can recognize ego states in yourself and others, you can not only change your own ego state, you can often get the other person to change his or her ego states.

For example, if an employee comes roaring at you with anger, criticizing you and telling you what you and the company are doing wrong, you have several choices. One, you can out-Parent him and order him to shut up. Two, you may go to your Child ego state and feel almost speechless with fear. Three, you may go to your Adult ego state and look for a way to get him to join you in his Adult. As a sample, you might wait until he takes a breath and then begin probing for facts, realizing that in his Parent ego state he is delivering opinions and perhaps prejudices. You will not do this smoothly and efficiently, however, unless you can recognize ego states both in yourself and in others.

RECOGNITION OF EGO STATES

In later chapters, we teach some techniques useful in getting others to change their ego states. First, though, you must learn to recognize these various ego states. There are three primary ways to do this:

1. The behavior of the individual
   a) verbal communication
   b) nonverbal communication

2. Social response of other persons to the individual

3. History.

The Behavior of an Individual

Many people tend to think that they can recognize ego states
by the words people use. While these words are so important
that we provide a list of them in Fig. 4, our belief is that words
constitute the smaller part of the communication between two
people. Indeed, some studies show that as little as 7 percent
of the communication between people is in words, 45 percent
is in the tone in which the words are spoken, and 48 percent
is transmitted nonverbally. Think of some instances when you
have heard people insult each other. If you wrote the words
down on paper, they might not sound so bad. Spit them out
with a biting anger, a snarled face, and a clenched fist and the
diagnosis is easy to make. Remember the last time someone
shook their finger in your face? You probably didn't like it.
You may have gone into your Child ego state and wanted to

	Physical (Nonverbal)	Verbal
PARENT	The pointing finger, shaking head, handwringing, arms folded across the chest, foot tapping, wrinkled brow, pursed lips, sighing, impatient snort, grunts. A comforting touch, consoling sounds, holding and rocking, patting a person on the shoulder.	Always, never, remember, you ought to know better. You should do better. Don't. Now what, naughty, stupid, disgusting, how dare you, shocking, asinine, absurd, ridiculous, horrid. Poor thing, dear, sonny, honey, there, there. Cute, try again, don't worry. Unthinking, *evaluative* reactions of all types.

	Physical (Nonverbal)	Verbal
ADULT	Lively facial expressions. Listening, appropriate responses to what the other person is saying. Concerned, interested appearance and posture. Relaxed calm when appropriate, vigorous "body english" when appropriate.	Why, what, where, when, who, how. Alternatives, possible, probably, relatively. Identification of opinion as an opinion (not fact). Restating what the other person said and identifying it as a restatement to check understanding.
CHILD	Flirtatious behavior. Giggling, teasing, squirming, bubbling. Hand raised for permission to speak. Tears, pouting, temper tantrums, whining tone, quivering lip. No answer, biting lower lip, downcast eyes, nail biting, shrugging shoulder.	Wow! Gee whiz! I love you. Baby talk. Didn't I do good? Mine's bigger than yours. Please help me. I wish. I want. I dunno. I'll try. I don't care. Look at me. Nobody loves me. MINE! NOW! Back biting *after* other person has left the room. Can't. Won't.

Fig. 4 Clues to Parent, Adult, and Child behavior

bite the finger. Accordingly, in Fig. 4, we have also listed some of the important nonverbal communications people transmit when they are in their different ego states.

Social Response of Others to the Individual

When Bill came back to work after burying his mother, many people tried to comfort him. Some used words; some put their hand on his shoulder as they spoke to him. They recognized the sad Child ego state in him and responded from their Nurturing Parent. If you go to one of your subordinates and are in your Critical Parent ego state, the subordinate is very likely to go into his Child ego state and not hear much that you say.

We can learn a great deal about ego states by watching people as they transact their daily business. The manager is often in the position of using his or her Parent ego state to control, criticize, regulate, and lead. If the manager leads entirely from the Critical Parent ego state, as in Theory X, he or she is not likely to get much work done, since the ego state that matches the Parent is another Parent ego state or a Child ego state. Much work must be done from the Adult. Adult behavior on the part of one person invites such behavior on the part of another.

History

If Max says about his boss, "He bosses just like my Dad did. Never listens," then he is using his own personal life history to help him put the boss in the Parent slot. However, if your secretary acts too much like your mother did, you are likely to feel in your Child ego state, just like you did when you were little and Mom insisted you wear your raincoat and overshoes when you really didn't want to.

CONTAMINATION

Sometimes we are puzzled as to the ego state a person is actually using. Such confusions are especially likely to arise when the person says something, believing it to be a fact, while you hear it as an opinion or a feeling. In such instances, we say that the individual has a contamination, or *leak*, from one ego state into another. In Fig. 5, the person might be saying, "Nice children don't do things like that," while literally looking down his nose. He believes he is stating a fact. Actually, the Parent in him is expressing a value judgment, an opinion, or perhaps the command, "Stop it!" This is a technique that we call "mind-bending"—i.e., presenting a command as a fact. Many managers use this technique with employees. In Fig. 6, the person may be saying, "I'll move to another company where everyone is always happy and cooperative, and they'll treat me right." The person is expressing as fact what is actually a wish from the Child to have someone literally *make* him or her happy!*

Fig. 5 Contamination: prejudice

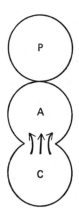

Fig. 6 Contamination: delusion

---

*Incidentally, we believe it is impossible to *make* anyone happy. We can only go so far as to help, not *cause* happiness in someone else.

In contaminations, the person does not use his or her Adult to look at facts in the light of today, but instead looks at them through the eyes of the Parent or of the Child. Consequently, they are out of date, since these recordings were made long ago. The job of the Adult is to monitor feelings and other inputs from both the Child and the Parent, as well as from outside the person, then evaluate these facts realistically. When we deal with an individual with leaks or contaminations such as these, our efforts are directed toward getting the person's Adult back in gear and separating feelings from facts. Fig. 5 represents prejudice, literally a prejudging before the fact. It makes no difference whether it is a racial or religious prejudice, or someone in business who says, "We've always run this company this way," while meaning, "I know the right way to run this company. Don't come around here criticizing me, you little upstart." At best, Fig. 6 represents a fantasy that the person almost insists will come true; at worst, it represents a delusion. The only problem with wishes and fantasies is finding a way to make them come true, if possible. With delusions, the individual literally doesn't know what is real from what is not. Such cases call for a clinically trained therapist, not an on-the-job adjustment by the manager.

The interactions of ego states within an individual can be a scourge or a blessing. The manager of a company who is tempted to "buy" business through bribery or kickbacks may have a strong Parent that says, "Don't! It's not right." This is diagrammed in Fig. 7, arrow (a). Such monitoring is an important function of the Critical Parent ego state, which serves as a guide to, or monitor of, value systems held by the individual. The Nurturing Parent that gives support when the manager is faced with a difficult business problem (e.g., "Don't give up. You can solve that problem.") provides managerial persistence in the face of obstacles. We'll use dotted lines to

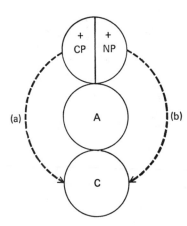

Fig. 7 OK Parenting

show internal relationships of this kind as in Fig. 7, arrow (b). After the alert is given by either aspect of the Parent to the Child, it is the task of the Adult to check facts and find the best way to handle the situation at hand while winning approval of the Parent and gratifying the Child, if possible.

On the other hand, the person with an overactive Critical Parent heaping abuse on his or her Child ego state (see Fig. 8) may hear such messages as, "That's good, but it's not good enough. . . . A thing worth doing at all is worth doing well. . . . Yes, you have done well to become the manager, now why aren't you the President?" If the manager pays more attention to these influences from the Critical Parent than he or she does to Adult facts, depression may result. This outcome could require professional help.

The significant fact is: many, perhaps most, managers have more than an average amount of Parent-ego-state activity. If they did not, they probably would never have chosen to be-

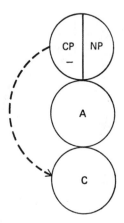

Fig. 8 Not-OK Critical Parent

come managers. You need to utilize the okay aspects of your Parent, both Critical and Nurturing, in constructive ways to help your superiors (yes, even your superiors), subordinates, and associates learn, grow, and become productive, self-actualizing people who can find satisfaction in their work. Unfortunately, some managers appear to have an excess of Critical Parent which is not well received by their associates, as shall become clearer in the next chapter.

At first glance, some managers appear to be nothing but pure Adult. They do not seem to have any fun nor to be interested in the fun, welfare, or feelings of others. They are excellent with detail and poor when it comes to leading others to work. Many such managers often receive messages from the Parent in their heads telling them such things as, "Life is serious. . . . Work for the night cometh. . . . Hard work never hurt anybody." Such managers are not much fun to work with or for.

Some individuals, when promoted to the position of manager, act suddenly as if they are much older Parents whose job it is to see that people become serious and no longer have any fun. Actually, such managers are often operating out of a scared Adapted Child position. Paying some attention to what the Adult requirements of the job are, using the Parent to tell him or her about what others need for their growth, and using the Child to promote fun while at work may make the person a much better manager.

DIAGRAM ANALYSIS

Reviewing the ego-state diagram, Fig. 3, page 14, we can rotate it counterclockwise 90 degrees to provide a basic diagram for analyzing the extent of the individual's ego states (Fig. 9).

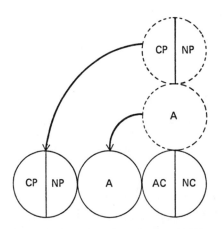

Fig. 9 Rotation of ego state diagram

Using the horizontal line-up of ego states that results (Fig. 10), an egogram can be drawn on which you can construct a bar graph indicating a rough estimate of how you see yourself. The solid lines indicate your estimate of how you see yourself dealing with others; dotted lines may be drawn in the Critical Parent and Nurturing Parent columns to indicate how your Parent treats the Adult and Child ego states in you.

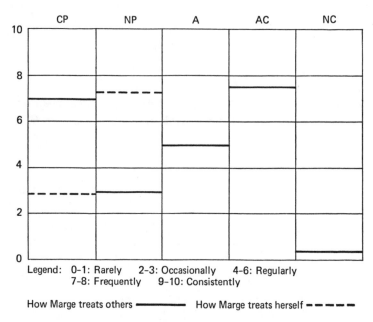

Legend: 0-1: Rarely   2-3: Occasionally   4-6: Regularly
         7-8: Frequently   9-10: Consistently

How Marge treats others —————— How Marge treats herself ▬ ▬ ▬ ▬ ▬

Fig. 10 Egogram analysis: Marge Martin, manager

In the diagram (Fig. 10), Marge, the manager, believes she is frequently seen by associates as Critical Parent, occasionally as Nurturing Parent, regularly in her Adult, frequently in her Adapted Child, and rarely in her Natural Child. The dotted lines in the Critical Parent column indicate she believes she treats herself only occasionally from her Critical Parent and frequently from her Nurturing Parent. Essentially, she sees herself as more critical of others than of herself, and more forgiving and supportive of herself than she is of others.* This is not an unusual pattern in managers, but the question is: Does this create the optimal conditions for productivity and cooperation in the organization?

Marge can make some changes in this pattern if she wishes. One route is through awareness of how she treats herself and others, plus the setting of a few personal behavioral-change objectives. Another route is to join a competently led group that seeks to accomplish some individual growth in a group setting.

SUMMARY

One of the important skills to be learned in applying TA concepts to oneself and others is to identify ego states quickly and accurately. When a person speaks, the big question is: Who's doing the talking? Parent, Adult, or Child ego state? If Parent, is it Nurturing or Critical Parent? If Child, is it Natural or Adapted Child? The manager and the subordinate need not open their mouths to communicate. Remember to look for what is being communicated by the *kinesics*, the nonverbal postures, gestures, facial expressions, and voice tones. All the right words in the world will not get your message across unless they are accompanied by the proper "music." For example, if you use words praising an individual's work, but ac-

---

*Actually, the way the Parent in your head treats you is likely to be the way you treat others, even though you bend over backwards not to treat them that way.

company these words with a scowl, a frown, and pulling away from the person, that individual is likely to know that you do not mean what you are saying.

When two people are transacting—exchanging messages—the resulting communication can be very simple and straightforward ("coming on straight") or very complex. The consequences of the communication can be improved relationships and productive cooperation or just the opposite, as we discuss in the next chapter.

SUGGESTED ACTIVITIES

1. Identify one of your personal prejudices based primarily on recordings in your Parent ego state. How did you acquire this recording? From a parent? If so, which parent? Do you remember specific incidents, conversations, or phrases often expressed by that parent which provided the recording?

2. Review the verbal and nonverbal clues to the Child ego state in Fig. 4. Can you identify instances when you were in your Child ego state on the job...off the job? How did you feel? How did others respond? Did your Child behavior affect your relationship with others? How?

3. In Fig. 4, the "pointing finger" is said to identify a Parent ego state—specifically, a Critical Parent ego state. Can you think of a situation where the pointing finger would be used by the Adult ego state? By the Child ego state? When do you use the pointing finger? What effect does it have on your subordinates? Associates? Family members?

4. When would it be okay for you to be in your Child ego state on the job?

5. a) List some directions or advice your actual parents gave you which are still good rules to live by.
   b) List some that are no longer appropriate.

6. Refer to the explanation of an egogram on page 24. In the figure below, draw your own egogram based on the way you think you actually function, i.e., actually "come on" with other people in your daily pursuits and encounters. Use the legend provided and draw a graph representing *your* egogram. Remember, the time spent in an ego state is only relative. Use the words "frequently," "occasionally," etc., as you understand them; you do *not* have to make the total of the five columns equal 10.

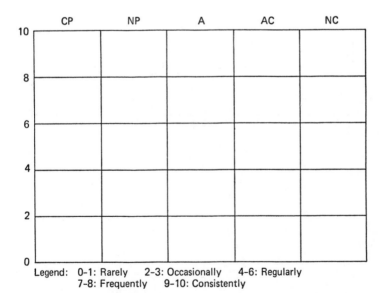

Legend: 0-1: Rarely   2-3: Occasionally   4-6: Regularly
         7-8: Frequently   9-10: Consistently

Your Egogram—Actual

Would you like to change the frequency with which you are in any of the five ego states? If you have an ideal egogram that might improve the quality of your life or your encounters with others, draw it in the graph below.

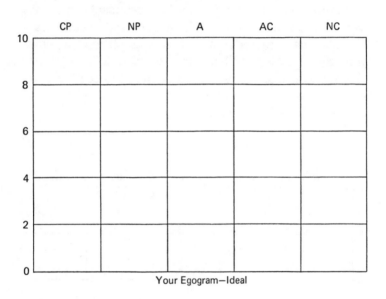

Your Egogram—Ideal

3

It's Your Move!

The early pioneer in TA, Dr. Eric Berne, was fond of games and described much of what goes on between people as a series of moves or plays. In gin rummy, one person plays a card, the other person picks up one card and plays another, and so on until the final play is completed. A transaction is much the same. A person sends a message, the message is received by a second person who then sends back a message, in turn received by the first person. Thus, two people and from two to four ego states are directly involved. This clip, blip, or unit of human interaction is termed a transaction, and the diagnosis of such transactions is known as transactional analysis.

In any organization, and depending on the total number of people, thousands of transactions take place every day—perhaps every hour. Sometimes the outcomes seem favorable, communications are clear, people enjoy the work and each other. In many cases, the opposite is true—miscommunication causes misdirected effort, loss of energy through bad feelings, and lowered morale and productivity.

For example: A manager has just completed conducting a performance review with a subordinate who has enjoyed generally good success on the job for the past year. At the conclusion, both persons are angry, upset, and feel frustrated with each other.

Their problem is not so much a matter of personality clash, ill will, or dislike for the other as it is ignorance and unawareness of how their transactions are causing communication blocks.

Perhaps the best way of understanding transactional analysis is to look at various examples of transactions, then diagram them according to standard analytical procedures. For consistency, the originating, or sending message will be drawn as starting from an ego state of the individual on the left and impacting on an ego state of the individual on the right. The response will be drawn with arrows proceeding from right to left.

COMPLEMENTARY TRANSACTIONS

The first general category of transactions includes those in which the lines of the diagram are parallel. These are described as complementary transactions, and the first law of transactional analysis states: When the lines of a diagram are parallel, communication *can* continue. Communication may *not* continue, but it *can* continue.

Figure 11 depicts a Parent-Parent transaction. The two presidents are "parenting" each other, and they are in apparent agreement as to their value judgements about unions. They could go on like this for many minutes, or they might smile and nod and move on to another person, another transaction.

Complementary transactions

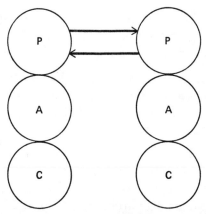

XYZ Company president: (at cocktail party) "Unions are just getting far too powerful these days."

ABC Company president: (replying) "They sure are! They're a prime cause of inflation, which has ruined our economy!"

Fig. 11   Parent-Parent transaction

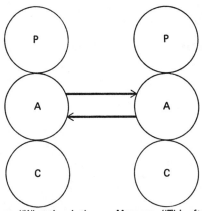

Employee: "What time is the staff meeting today?"

Manager: "This afternoon at three o'clock."

Fig. 12   Adult-Adult transaction

In Fig. 12, an Adult-Adult complementary transaction, a question is asked and a specific answer is received. There is no emotional or feeling content apparent in the interchange.

The two management trainees in Fig. 13 are attending a university management seminar and are having so much fun they want to keep celebrating on into the night—a Child-to-Child complementary transaction.

In Fig. 14, employee$_1$ tosses out an unhappy, rebellious, defensive comment, probably not caring where it lands, perhaps as much to himself as to anyone else. Wonder of all wonders, a co-worker responds with an offer to help! A Child-Parent complementary transaction has occurred, in which Bill will

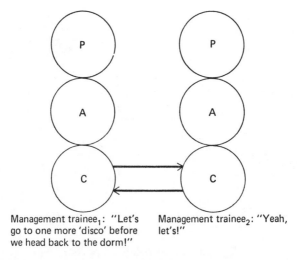

Management trainee$_1$: "Let's go to one more 'disco' before we head back to the dorm!"

Management trainee$_2$: "Yeah, let's!"

Fig. 13 Child-Child transaction

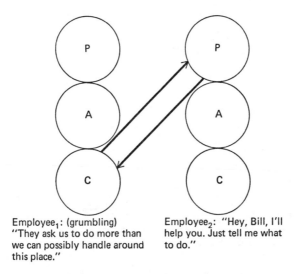

Employee₁: (grumbling)
"They ask us to do more than
we can possibly handle around
this place."

Employee₂: "Hey, Bill, I'll
help you. Just tell me what
to do."

Fig. 14 Child-Parent transaction

probably next brighten up and ask for help with a certain part of his assignment.

The exact same stimulus, or sending message, could, however, elicit a somewhat different response from the co-worker, as diagrammed in Fig. 15. This interaction is still complementary; the two employees could go to the rest room, light up cigarettes, and cuss and discuss the deficiencies of the outfit for which they are working. The social response of the second employee aids in analyzing the transaction accurately.

In the next transaction (Fig. 16), the sales manager, Ed Davis, is making calls with one of his sales representatives, Joan Blake. During an interview with a purchasing agent, Ed has taken over to close an important sale. The agent has asked a question about deliveries, indicating a two-week date would be

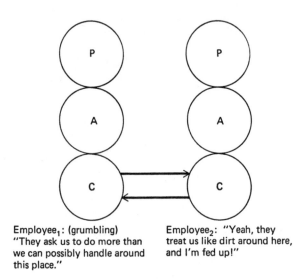

Employee₁: (grumbling)
"They ask us to do more than
we can possibly handle around
this place."

Employee₂: "Yeah, they
treat us like dirt around here,
and I'm fed up!"

Fig. 15   Child-Child transaction

necessary. Joan, who had earlier determined that the factory
would not have items ready to ship for four weeks, interrupted
the conversation to point out this "fact" to her boss, Ed, and
the buyer. The purchasing agent refused to sign an order for
the material on the basis of a four-week delivery date and Ed
and Joan withdrew to their car where the Fig. 16 transaction
took place.

The hunched shoulders and pleading eyes of the sales representative pinpoint her response as Child, and the transaction is
Parent-Child. The sales representative has "adapted." She becomes Child to placate her boss and mollify his temper. It is a
complementary transaction. Communication lines are open
and communication will continue as long as the two wish to
continue with their complementary roles.

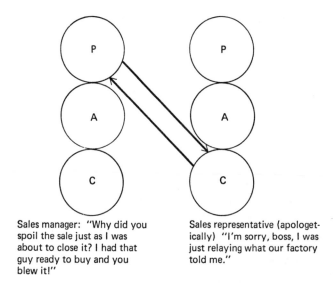

Sales manager: "Why did you spoil the sale just as I was about to close it? I had that guy ready to buy and you blew it!"

Sales representative (apologetically) "I'm sorry, boss, I was just relaying what our factory told me."

Fig. 16 Parent-Child transaction

CROSSED TRANSACTIONS

Still, given the same stimulus, the same put-down approach as in Fig. 16, the response could conceivably come from an entirely different ego state.

Figure 17 illustrates a truly "crossed spears" transaction. The second law of transactional analysis is: When the lines of the transactional diagram cross, it is a crossed transaction, and communication will stop.

Remember, *communication* will stop, but "noise" can continue. In Fig. 17, the boss may raise his voice level, get redder in the face, and escalate the exchange to a point of no return for both individuals. They might continue the feud for an ex-

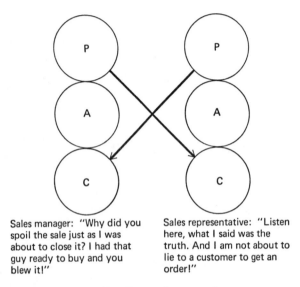

Sales manager: "Why did you spoil the sale just as I was about to close it? I had that guy ready to buy and you blew it!"

Sales representative: "Listen here, what I said was the truth. And I am not about to lie to a customer to get an order!"

Fig. 17 Crossed transaction

tended period of time and it could ultimately result in Joan's transfer or even resignation.

Other forms of crossed transactions are less explosive on the surface, but just as disturbing to interpersonal relations. In Fig. 18, the Chief's statement is heavily Critical Parent and probably exaggerated due to use of the word "always." The transaction could have been kept complementary and opened up a discussion of alternatives to overtime if the Chief had stayed in his Adult and asked, "Is there some way we can get it finished without it costing us fifteen hours of overtime and three suppers?"

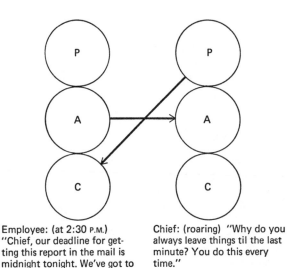

Employee: (at 2:30 p.m.)
"Chief, our deadline for getting this report in the mail is
midnight tonight. We've got to
keep three typists overtime
until ten o'clock to get it
finished."

Chief: (roaring) "Why do you
always leave things til the last
minute? You do this every
time."

Fig. 18 Crossed transaction

In Fig. 19, the sending message is straight Adult, factual in
words and tone. Reviewing Fig. 4 again, you can pick out the
two words in the response that designate it as Child. First is
the word "can't." Second is the word "thirteen," which is usually in the class of "million" or "zillion." The only way the response could be classified as Adult is if employee$_2$ could produce a list of thirteen "to do" items that had been specified by
the individual's boss to accomplish before taking on any other
assignment. The chances of this are, to say the least, remote.

The last crossed transaction to be illustrated (Fig. 20) involves
two Child ego states. The tired whine in both voices, the help-

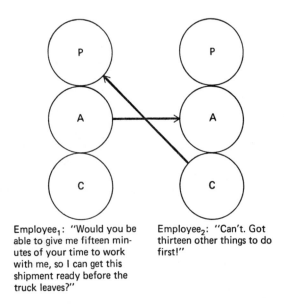

Employee₁: "Would you be able to give me fifteen minutes of your time to work with me, so I can get this shipment ready before the truck leaves?"

Employee₂: "Can't. Got thirteen other things to do first!"

Fig. 19 Crossed transaction

less looks, the plea for assistance places both messages in the Child ego state. Help has been asked for, and help has not been given. It's a crossed transaction. Both will probably turn back to their typewriters and feel worse than before.

ULTERIOR TRANSACTIONS

The third general classification of transactions is "ulterior," involving a total of three or more ego states. An ulterior transaction has a hidden meaning; what is really going on is different from what appears to be going on. An ulterior motive may be present, as in the case of the salesman showing a selection of

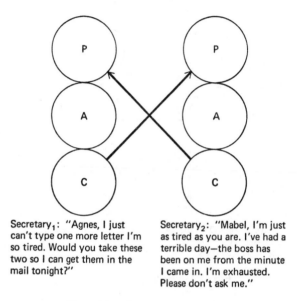

Secretary₁: "Agnes, I just can't type one more letter I'm so tired. Would you take these two so I can get them in the mail tonight?"

Secretary₂: "Mabel, I'm just as tired as you are. I've had a terrible day—the boss has been on me from the minute I came in. I'm exhausted. Please don't ask me."

Fig. 20 Crossed transaction

suits to an obviously "fortyish" prospective customer, depicted in Fig. 21.

On the surface, the salesman is stating in factual tones his opinion of the suit he is showing; actually, however, he is appealing to the Child ego state of a middle-years buyer. Assuming the customer's response is from the Natural Child, it could be either a fun-loving, OK Natural Child ("Wow, I'm a swinger, all right!") or an "I'll show you," not-OK rebellious Natural Child. From the words alone, we can't tell which; we need to hear the tone and see the posture, gestures, and facial expressions to diagnose which ego state is responding. It would be fairly obvious the reply is from the Adult if the customer re-

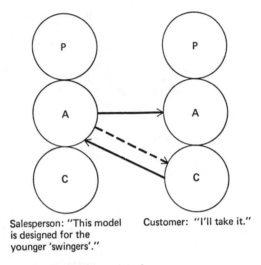

Salesperson: "This model   Customer: "I'll take it."
is designed for the
younger 'swingers'."

Fig. 21   Angular transaction

sponded factually, "I'm tending to get a bit thick in the middle and I doubt that the fitted design would be best for me."

When three ego states are involved, the ulterior transaction is "angular." When four ego states are involved at once, the transaction is "duplex." Flirting, double-meaning jokes, and private jokes can be diagrammed as in Fig. 22. In this case, the hidden, or ulterior, meaning reveals the true nature of the relationship. However, neither party is deeply committed to the transaction and either one can call a halt to the proceedings at any time.

OTHER TRANSACTIONS

A transaction may not be completed in a communication sense when only one sending and one responding message

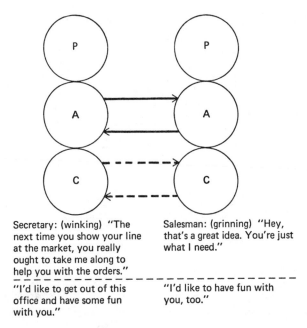

Secretary: (winking) "The next time you show your line at the market, you really ought to take me along to help you with the orders."

Salesman: (grinning) "Hey, that's a great idea. You're just what I need."

"I'd like to get out of this office and have some fun with you."

"I'd like to have fun with you, too."

Fig. 22 Duplex transaction

have been exchanged. The transaction may be a continuing one with three or more "moves" being executed. We believe the "third move," in many cases, determines the real nature of the continuing relationship between two people. The authenticity of a relationship is revealed more by the response of the sender to the response of the responder than by any other element. The visualization of the third move is readily diagrammed. Figure 23 shows a Sender originating an A⟶A transaction, which for whatever reason evoked a belligerent Child response. The big question is: What will be the nature of the response of the Sender to this response of the Responder? The diagram illustrates it as an A⟶A, with a number 3 in the arrow to indicate "third move."

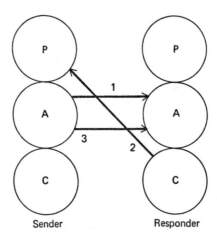

Fig. 23 "Third-move" diagram

Let's put the essence of the notion in narrative form first, before we fit dialogue to the figure. The idea of authenticity is best described in the first person, when I say, "The essence of my relationship to you is best demonstrated in my response to your response to me."

> *Example:* If, as an interested associate, I seek to give you input on a technical problem and you respond with instant criticism in a superior, contemptuous manner, the true relationship is revealed in what I do next. Do I go to my vengeful Child and withdraw to let you get your own ideas? Or to my equally contemptuous critical Parent to do battle over our technical, doctrinal differences? Or do I respond from an OK nurturing Parent?...or even from my OK Critical Parent?...or reflective Adult?...or my caring, affiliative Child?

Let's analyze the third move using a TA interpretation to describe the situation of "authenticity."

Constancy as authenticity. Figure 23 illustrates the diagram of the constancy element in authenticity. The sequence could be:

1. *Shipping coordinator (factually)*: "What happened to the order for Carlton Corporation? It was supposed to be ready to ship this afternoon."

2. *Production supervisory (belligerently)*: "You just tend to your business, I'll tend to mine!"

3. *Shipping coordinator:* "Look, I'm not trying to tend to your business. The main question is, What needs to be done to get it out tonight?"

The shipping coordinator sensed the defensive attitude of the production supervisor, not only by the words, but by the protruding lower lip, chin-down position of the head, and the rebellious tone. The coordinator did not respond either from a superior, abusive Parent, nor did he get "hooked" into an equally rebellious, "yah-yah" Child-to-Child encounter. Instead, he came back in his Adult and responded with *constancy* from his original Adult ego state.

Positive, cooperative responses as authenticity. Returning to Fig. 23, the third move could have been diagrammed as shown in Fig. 24 and given this dialogue:

1. *Manager (to employee)*: "How's it going?"

2. *Employee (with feeling)*: "Okay, okay. Hey, keep off my back, will you? If I don't get it done today, I'll finish it tomorrow. Okay?"

3. *Manager (smiling)*: "Hey, you really are up tight. Let me give you a lift; you just tell me what to do and I'll pitch in. The boss wants this ready the first thing tomorrow and we really should complete it tonight."

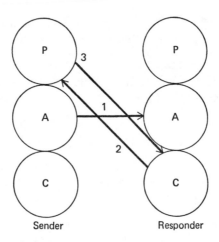

Fig. 24 "Third-move" diagram

Here, the manager responds to a not-so-OK Child response of the employee with a good-feeling, sincere Nurturing Parent. If the employee will accept the positive offer of cooperation in good spirit, the communication channels will be open and the complementary transactions can continue. The key here is an OK complementary response to the not-OK original response of the employee. This is the Biblical returning of "good" for "bad"; it is authenticity in action.

Growth responses as authenticity. When the third move is aimed toward helping the Responder grow, become, expand skills, or develop healthier mental attitudes and life positions, it builds toward authentic relationships between the two persons.

Trainer: "Now, let me check you out on this operation to make sure you really have mastered it."

New Employee (discouraged face and tone): "The trouble is I haven't. . .and I don't think I ever will. (*Shakes head.*) I'm just not cut out for this job. I guess I better quit while the quitting is good."

Trainer: "The fact is you're about at the same stage as any other employee who trained on this job. This is the low point for most people I've trained. Stick with it. You can make it. Now, let's go over it again."

The trainer's response to the discouragement of the employee was mostly Adult with some Nurturing Parent in evidence. But, it doesn't matter whether the third move is from the Parent, Adult, or Child *if* it gets the employee to grow in skill and confidence.

YOUR CHOICES

The encouraging part about TA is the hope it holds out for improving communications between people. You don't have to be at the mercy of your not-OK Child or Parent ego state; you can do something constructive when you become aware of the situation and your options. When you are on the receiving end of a message (you are the Responder), here is a "program" to run through your Adult computer.

On receipt of the stimulus or sending message, ask yourself:

1. What is the other person's ego state? Remember to consider verbal and nonverbal behaviors, the ego state in yourself which seems to be invited to respond, and where you think the Sender aimed the stimulus.

2. What is that person's need? To achieve—to be autono-
   mous—to be "right" (this time)—to be needed—to be re-
   spected?

3. How should I respond?

   a) Go to my Adult? Will this really help the situation or the
      person?
   b) Shall I stroke the other person?
      —From which ego state should I stroke—from my
      Parent, my Adult, or my Child?
      —Which ego state in the other person most needs the
      stroke—Parent, Adult, or Child?
   c) Should I stay complementary? Keep the lines parallel and
      communication open? Or would this mean continuing an
      unhealthy or an unrewarding relationship?
   d) Should I cross the sending message—with the hope that
      a more fruitful level of transaction could be initiated?

If you decide to cross a transaction because it seems unproductive to continue the pattern of the original transaction, you
must plan what kind of transaction would be more productive.
When you have made a diagnosis and plan, invite the Sender
to make the third move from the most appropriate of the three
ego states by proceeding as follows.

To invite the Sender to move to Adult:

1. Ask a question.

2. Make an Adult statement. . .state some facts.

3. Ask for options and for the other person's preference. The
   best management questions that can be asked of a subordinate are, "What are our options?" and "What is your
   recommendation?"

To invite the person to move to the Nurturing Parent:

1. Ask for help: "Boss, I don't think I can handle this problem alone; I need your help."

2. Communicate your fears about the situation (if you have them) to the other person.

3. Ask for advice. To the customer who has a complaint ask, "What would you think a fair adjustment would be? What would you do if you were in our place?"

To invite a person to move to the Natural Child:

1. Be one yourself—joke, "cut up," have fun.

2. Show the fun side of the situation; say, "Maybe we could have more fun out of this if we'd move the Board meeting this year to Bermuda!"

3. Be a Nurturing Parent; say, "I'd like to help...if I can...and if you want me to help."

4. Be enthusiastic; share your excitement with the other person.

5. Show a new or fresh way of looking at the *old* things; say, "Hey, let's look at this advertisement for cat food from a different angle. How about looking at All Crab Meat Cat Food from the viewpoint of a cat? What would we like about it—how would we react the first time we sniffed it?"

The first time you use this new "computer program," it will seem a bit time consuming. However, with continued practice, it will become second nature. You will find yourself increasingly able to bring out the OK Nurturing Parent, the OK Natural Child, or the Adult ego states in others. Try it...you'll like the improved results that can be obtained.

SUMMARY

Many of the cross-ups in communications within organizations are due to ignorance and unawareness of the powerful influence of transactions on communication outcomes. Complementary, crossed, and ulterior transactions can be diagrammed to better predict what will happen when two people encounter each other. A complementary transaction suggests that communication channels are open and communication can continue; a crossed transaction signifies that communication will stop—at that level—but that a more successful transaction can be initiated by one who is familiar with methods of moving others toward complementary types of transactions. Ulterior transactions are the most difficult for the uninitiated to understand. These transactions always have a hidden meaning different from the ostensible, or apparent, meaning.

Authenticity is characterized by a genuine, meaningful relationship between any two people. The truly authentic relationship is established most clearly by the response of one person to the response of the other to some initial behavior of the first person. This is termed the "third move." The three types of third moves which can establish authenticity are: (1) constancy; (2) positive, cooperative; and (3) growth-oriented.

The great advantage of applying transactional analysis lies in the matter of choices. Individuals have an opportunity to deliberately select the response they wish to make to a stimulus, or sending message. Pausing to examine briefly the sender and his or her message, the responder can choose the mode of response best calculated to bring about both improved relationships and results in the organization.

SUGGESTED ACTIVITIES

1. You have requested an employee to do an errand that is within the requirements of his job description. In a quarrelsome, whiney voice, he reacts with: "Why do you pick on me to do the dirty jobs?" At the same time, he shrugs his shoulders and turns his palms up in a gesture of helplessness. What ego state is he most likely in? What would be an Adult response from you? A Child response? A Parent response? Which ego-state(s) responses would most likely cross his response? What is the response from you most likely to result in good feelings on both your parts? Check this out with one of your trusted employees.

2. A manager who works closely with you is a very likeable person and you work well together. He has considerable prejudice about minority workers. You don't agree but you haven't expressed yourself on the subject. One of his minority subordinates has just "goofed" in handling an important matter and the manager comes over to tell you about it, probably to enlist your sympathy. "These blankety-blank 'ethnics' around here are no damn good to themselves or anybody else" is his lead-in statement. You know he expects you to sympathize and agree with his bias, but you feel that you should take a stand for fair play for the minorities in the organization. What response from which of your ego states would have the best chance of creating a creative, positive-thinking response in your associate? Write down actual words...say them aloud...decide what gestures or facial expressions would best support the message you are trying to convey. Check this out with a fellow manager.

3. A manager stops by her secretary's desk with a couple of pieces of paper in her hand and inquires, "Where did you hide the stapler?" What kind of a message is being conveyed by the manager? From which ego state(s) could the secretary respond? Write a response for each ego state you have listed in answer to the previous question. From which ego state is the secretary most likely to respond?

4. You are a half-hour late in arriving to work one morning. Your boss greets you with a sarcastic, "Good afternoon!" Make up a response from each of your three ego states which would be likely to promote a good-feeling relationship between the two of you.

4

Having the Time of Your Life!

Bill Remey is a tough-minded, hard-nosed manager who is always driving himself, and others, to ever-higher accomplishments. Unfortunately, he is seen by several of his subordinates as more of a "snoopervisor" than a supervisor. He seems to be always trying to catch them in an error. . . trying to get the "goods" on someone. He is hypercritical and more than ordinarily suspicious of how his people use their time. An overlong coffee break or an extra-long lunch hour brings a glower to his face. Some of the time, his subordinates feel guilty, even though they can't think of anything specific they may have done to invite his disfavor. Six months ago, he fired his administrative assistant with the comment that the assistant was a "pure d--- loafer." No one in the office sees any realistic reason for this firing. Some think he did it just to make an example of the assistant so other employees would "shape up." Bill is a hard and sincere worker. To understand why he acts as he does, let's look at six ways in which people spend their time.

ACTIVITIES

Time is perceived in many different ways. Some believe, as
Ben Franklin stated, that "time is money," and the phrase
"spend time" is a natural evolution of that concept. Many of
us have been schooled for years in how to "invest" our time,
so it is not surprising that people in a Western civilized society
prize *activities*. Activities are project-oriented and include
studying, working, problem solving, housekeeping, creating
ideas, building structures and concepts, teaching, and other
useful activities that advance work. For a large part of our
waking hours, most of us deal with the realities of the business
of living. However, activities do not *require* us to have *intimate* involvement with others.

WITHDRAWAL

Sometimes, we tire of activities. We withdraw for rest and re-
freshment. We periodically like to "get away from it all" on a
vacation or an occasional weekend. Withdrawal is important to
all of us. When we withdraw from people, we do not transact;
it can even happen in a social situation. It may be an escape
into fantasy when the conversation is boring or the discussion
seems unimportant to the person. The individual is physically
in the group, but mentally is somewhere else where the stroking is better.

Lisa Minor is an intelligent, usually competent analyst working for Jack Meany, computer manager. Lately, she has become increasingly absentminded and forgetful. In despera-
tion, Jack has begun to hand her a tablet and pencil when
they sit down to discuss projects. Even so, when he pauses

halfway through what he is saying to inquire what her thinking is concerning his ideas, she frequently becomes flustered
and asks him to repeat. He knows her mind is not on her
job, and wonders how he can gracefully discuss the subject
with her without appearing to be too "personal."

Before Jack plans the strategy for his next interview with Lisa,
he should consider whether his approach is evoking this
response from Lisa. It need not be his approach; she may be
withdrawing for other reasons, e.g., preoccupation with other
work responsibilities, etc.

RITUALS

In a formal meeting, the Board of Directors are first called to
order, the minutes of the last meeting are read, reports are
made; then they are ready for old business, followed by new
business. When you greet a co-worker soon after arriving at
work, the greeting is predictably something like, "Hi, Bill." Rituals are stereotyped, predictable ways of spending time. They
include greetings, introductions, graduations. Dating and even
mating can become as highly stylized as rituals. If so, they will
be noted for the precision and predictability with which the
same moves are repeated. Rituals bring people together in a
loose fashion while providing them with plenty of distance
from each other.

Rituals are entirely acceptable ways of spending time. Like any
other of the ways of spending time, they may be inappropriate. For example, if all suggestions in the suggestion box are
ritualistically read, then discarded, the ritual is inappropriate. A
project-oriented activity, determining the usefulness of the suggestions, would be appropriate.

PASTIMES

The word pastime could have had either of two equally applicable beginnings. A pastime is usually "past in time"; it is also "passing the time." A pastime is a complementary transaction revolving around a single topic. When first acquainted, people tend to "pastime" at length on the weather, sports, automobiles, recipes, current news, and similar light topics about which knowledge is equally available to all. As people get better acquainted, the topics are less limited and are changed more rapidly. The socially adept generally enjoy pastiming; the "strictly business" type will not enjoy it for more than a very brief period of time. Pastiming has great merit as a beginning for two people, but indulging only in pastiming staves off intimacy, or deepening relationships. Pastiming has more stroke value than withdrawal, ritual, or activity, but those who receive most of their strokes this way usually have a stroke deficit.

Pastimes are great at coffee breaks and lunch. There, they appropriately add pleasure to our social contacts. However, if you are seeking agreement on a new way to increase efficiency in your department and someone begins to pastime about the "good old days when a man would really earn his wages," then pastiming is inappropriate.

GAMES

The fifth way of spending time gets closer to Bill Remey's problem—playing a *game*. Keep in mind there are many kinds of games—football games, chess games, golf games, card games, gambling games, party games, children's games—all of which are pleasurable to a degree, especially to the winner. In transactional analysis, a game has special meaning. The original definition by Dr. Berne was "an ongoing series of complementary, ulterior transactions, progressing to a well-defined, predictable outcome."

We believe TA games have three characteristics:

1. A bad payoff. TA games have a bad-feeling payoff for at least one person. Some end with bodily injury, even death.*

2. An ulterior or hidden quality. Therefore, a transactional diagram of a game will have the dashed line (see Fig. 26) to indicate that something other than what appears to be going on *is* going on.

3. Are played outside the awareness of the Adult ego states. The game initiator, and usually the person who is the object of the game, do not have Adult-ego-state awareness that a game is being played. If an individual is deliberately trying to manipulate another person, put him down, make him feel bad or inferior, we would term that activity a "ploy," not a game.

We regret that Berne chose the term *game* for this method of spending time. Like games in the sense of fun games, they may occupy a lot of time; indeed, they account for huge amounts of wasted time in business. Since psychological games have at least one loser, they are destructive of the win-win methods many managers want to use. From time to time, we all play some psychological games. Our Adult ego states are not always "plugged in." Skilled games players have been practicing since their youth.

---

*We differ from Berne in that we do not believe there are any good games.

In fact, the model for all psychological games can be found in childhood contests, such as "mine's better'n yours." The winner might not feel bad. The loser does. He may cry. He may pick up his toys and go home. When we see such contests in children, we know that one person will win while one loses. Games among grownups are somewhat harder to detect. With practice, such detection is easier. Recognizing them before the payoff saves a lot of bad feelings and a huge amount of time.

How, then, can you recognize a game? One of the best guidelines we know is this: You have probably been playing a game if you repeatedly feel bad at the end of an encounter with a certain person.

- Think now of an associate with whom this happens often.

- What ego state are you in when you have finished? Would you like to help or criticize from your Parent? Do you feel angry or embarrassed in your Child ego state?

What ego state was the initiator in at the beginning of the game? Once you know the ego state of the initiator, you can then look for the type of game most often played from that position. To do so, let's look at one way of classifying games.

Who Starts It—Parent or Child?

1. *Games played from the Parent Ego State*

Type 1 game is a favorite of some managers and is played out of a "heavy" Critical Parent. Bill Remey is probably playing a game known in TA circles as NIGYYSOB: "Now I've Got You, You S.O.B." The reasons for playing this game will be developed in more detail later in the chapter, but typically the

game could proceed as follows (we'll use the latest incident involving Bill Remey):

> The manager is meticulous about times of starting and stop-
> ping work, including rest breaks and lunch-hour obser-
> vances. His secretary is somewhat lax, in his opinion, in
> such matters and he gets upset each time a failure to live up
> to his standards occurs. One week, his secretary has been
> up to forty-five minutes late each day, due to her regular
> babysitter being sick and the need to scout around each
> morning to find a substitute. One Friday morning, the viola-
> tion occurs once more, with a twenty minute tardy appear-
> ance of Miss Jones.
>
> *Manager Remey:* "Oh, Miss Jones...I see you're late
> again."
>
> *Miss Jones:* "Oh, I'm so sorry, Mr. Remey, but my baby-
> sitter is still sick, and I had to get my sister-in-law to come
> over today to take care of the children. I'll be glad to work
> overtime to catch up, if need be. And I know my babysitter
> will be back next week."
>
> *Manager Remey:* "I'm sorry Miss Jones, but I just can't put
> up with your irregularity. I've already talked to Personnel
> about your transfer, and they would like to discuss the
> matter with you as soon as you can get over there."

We mercifully draw the scene to a close before the tears and
sobs start, and draw the transactional diagram shown in Fig.
25. The solid lines indicate the ostensible transaction, on an
Adult-Adult level. The dashed lines indicate the hidden message, in which Mr. Remey becomes "Top Dog" and momen-
tarily enjoys the luxury of his power play. The bad-feeling payoff is experienced by Miss Jones. The game ends, and the
stage is set for the next episode of "Mr. Remey Rules the
Roost."

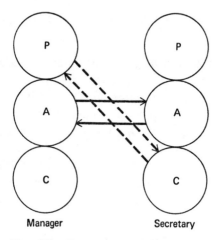

Fig. 25 Game initiated from Parent

Other games usually played out of a Critical Parent ego state and diagrammed similarly to the NIGYYSOB game are:

- *Blemish.* "That's nice, *but* did you notice this blemish?"

- *If It Weren't for You, Dumbbell.* "We'd have made our quota."

- *RAPO.* "Come on over, Charley, and play mudpies." When Charley does and gets dirty, she looks down on him and says, "You boys are all so dirty!"

- *Corner.* Initiator sets up a situation where you are cornered—you can't win whichever way you choose.

Games can be played from the Nurturing Parent position as well. The most common is: "I'm Only Trying to Help You." Since managers are in a position that inherently has some elements of the Parent in it, this game is a temptation for some managers, especially for those interested in the development of the individuals in their department.

In this game, the manager offers help which the individual has not requested. Whines and complaints—even tears—are not such requests; they are "hooks" for a game. After the manager does his or her best to help, the subordinate makes clear that that kind of help was not wanted. Then the manager may feel bad, thinking how much he or she wants to help the ungrateful subordinate. Such a game is diagrammed in the same way as Fig. 25. (Remember that the Parent ego state has both Critical and Nurturing functions.)

2. *Games played out of the Child ego state*

Type 2 games are a favorite of those who feel better if they can discount, or put down, associates whom they may envy or resent for one reason or another.

Let's listen in as a member of the secretary pool discusses a problem with other members of the pool during a rest break.

Jane: "You all may think you've got troubles, but I have a problem I don't know how to begin to do something about."

Carol: "What's that? Maybe we can help you."

Jane: "Well, I just don't have any dates, and I just don't seem to be able to do anything about it."

Carol: "Well, Jane, I think there's one thing that would really help. . .that's for you to lose some of that weight. Why don't you try Weight Watchers. . .it would make such a difference in your appearance."

Jane: "I know you're right, Carol, but that Weight Watchers diet just isn't for me. I tried it last year and didn't lose an ounce!"

Elaine: "Here's an idea, Jane. You've been letting your hair go. I personally believe you could attract more men if you got it styled and tinted a lighter shade. You'd be so attractive as a honey blonde."

Jane: "I thought of that, Elaine, but you know I have two children, and a dye job just costs too much for me to keep up. That's really out."

And on and on, until her associates get so frustrated with the discussion that one by one they slip away to more-important activities. Just as they reach that uptight point, you'll see a flicker of a Child smile of triumph as Jane says, "You women think you are so smooth, so cool, so smart. . . well, you aren't smart enough to help me!"

The diagram of this typical "Yes, But" game (Fig. 26) reveals the ostensible problem-solving Adult-Adult dialogue as well as the ulterior Child-Parent content.

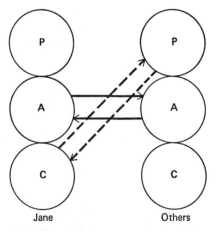

Fig. 26 Game initiated from Child

Other games usually diagrammed as in Fig. 26 and played out of the Child ego state are:

- *Kick Me.* The individual repeatedly sets up situations so that he or she is caught and, figuratively, kicked as though a Kick Me sign was pinned on the person's back without his or her knowledge. Example: A new women employee was warned that the company had a no-smoking rule everywhere in the plant except the lunch room. She was found smoking and warned. She said she'd forgotten. Two days later, as the manager walked by the ladies' rest room, the door opened. A cloud of smoke preceded the new employee out. She was surprised when he told her she was fired.

- *Stupid.* The stupid player is usually a smart person who acts stupid. When "caught" in "stupidity," the person may say, "I don't know why I can't figure that out. I must be stupid, I guess."

- *See What You Made Me Do?* This may be played by a secretary who angrily snatches a piece of paper from the typewriter while shooting a glance up at the manager who is standing too near for comfort. The secretary feels the manager *made* the mistake happen. At home, a father might hit his thumb with the hammer when the children are making noise and angrily say, "See what you made me do?" Of course, there is no way the children could make him hit his thumb with the hammer.

- *See How Hard I Try?* This may be played by the subordinate who almost always stays late, reads self-help books, and seems to work very hard. Much of this effort is spent on *looking* hard at work rather than actually spent in efficiently working hard.

- *Wooden Leg.* This is modeled on the person who says, "How do you expect me to run a race with this wooden leg?" In business, it may be seen when the manager asks for a specific piece of work to be completed that day and the subordinate feels something like, "How do you expect me to do that when I'm so worried about my marriage?"

- *Love Me No Matter What I Do.* This game is especially likely to be played by those still in their teens. Players put out one "bait" after another—this could include hair style and length, clothes style and length, tardiness—hoping that the manager will tell them to stop. Then they will try to convince the manager that he or she's an old-fashioned grump for not accepting them as they are.

- *Harried Executive.* This type manager keeps so busy with minute details that he or she always seems harried. People sometimes respond to this by feeling sorry for the manager and not asking him or her to do any more work. Over a short span of time, this may work. However, such a manager runs some risk of developing high blood pressure, as well as eventually wondering why some of the good jobs go to other workers.

Drama of Life Classifications

Games can also be classified according to the position on the drama triangle. (See Chapter 5, page 80, for an explanation of the drama triangle.) In each classification, the reinforcement of a life position is indicated, which gives a clue as to why the game is being played.

1. *Victim games*

These reinforce an "I'm Not OK" life position:

Kick Me	See How Hard I Try
Wooden Leg	See What You Made Me Do
Harried Executive	Love Me—No Matter What I Do
Stupid	

2. *Persecutor games*

These reinforce a "You're not OK" life position:

Blemish	If It Weren't for you, Dumbbell.
Corner	Now, I've Got You, You SOB
RAPO	Yes, But

3. *Rescuer games*

These reinforce a "You're Not OK" life position:

I'm Only Trying To Help You

Why People Play Games

With all the bad-feeling payoffs and frequent self-inflicted misery endured by the games player, it may seem a mystery why anyone would play games. The major reasons are:

1. Games are one of six ways to spend time. They are more exciting than many work activities or pastiming at the water cooler.

2. A game is a way to obtain familiar strokes. Even the "Kick Me" player must have negative strokes. After all, it is better to have negative strokes than to be ignored.

3. A game provides a familiar and predictable environment.

4. Although everyone wants intimacy, everyone also has some uneasiness about it. Some people make halfhearted attempts

at intimacy, then sabotage themselves by playing a game instead. Games do avoid intimacy.

5. Because the game supplies familiar strokes, it advances the life script . . . and reinforces a life position.

Game players experience some needs satisfaction at the conclusion of each game; the other person feels bad, or inadequate, or smaller, or discounted. The initiator has a fleeting moment of triumph over the other person.

How to Stop Games

The important need for managers is to know how to stop playing, particularly when they are the object of the game. The various methods of stopping a game are:

1. Confront it. Say, for example, "I feel bad—how can we do better?"

2. Ignore it—refuse to play the complementary hand.

3. Intuitive response—speak out honestly from Child ego state. Ask other person to do so. Level with him/her.

4. Refuse to take bad feeling. Stop discounting yourself *or* others.

5. Go back to your Adult. Get facts. Get the other to go Adult.

6. Ask yourself:

   a) How did it start?
   b) How did I miss knowing it was a game?
   c) Did I feel bad in my Parent or Child?

Other Ways to Deal with Games

In some cases you may not be able to "stop" games. You can alleviate their worst effects, however. An important way to do this is to determine which corner of the drama triangle the person is coming from. Then invite the person to go to another corner. This operates effectively in Alcoholics Anonymous where the alcoholic victim now goes to the Rescue corner and helps other alcoholics.

Similarly, in business, the Persecutor can often be induced to become a Rescuer by agreeing that he or she may be right in persecuting, judging, downgrading the other. Ask if he or she will help straighten that person out, not by chewing the individual out, since that won't work, but by finding other ways to help—perhaps a different job assignment, having the person report to the persecutor when the project is completed, asking his or her advice, etc.

INTIMACY

Intimacy is the most pleasant of all ways to spend time. Although in intimacy we find the greatest stroke value, it is difficult to define. When we speak of intimacy we mean a spontaneous, game-free, open way of relating to another person. These relationships are authentic; there are no cons, no put-ons, and no put-downs. When intimacy is present, fear is absent.

When we use the word intimacy, some people immediately think of sexual relations. Probably the most satisfying way to have sexual relations is genuinely intimate contact. However, sex can also be a ritual, a pastime on a rainy Sunday afternoon, or it can involve games, or be a withdrawal or an activity.

In intimacy, one is candid and speaks frankly to the partner. Some of you may have experienced a candid "opening up" in intimate fashion while talking to a seatmate on an airplane, knowing full well that you will never see that person again. At the end of the flight, you may be amazed that you have told so much about yourself and felt so comfortable in the process. When people are intimate, they almost always show their Natural Child and/or their Nurturing Parent (Critical Parent may also be present, as in a righteous anger).

Some people believe that only a precious few hours or even minutes in a lifetime can actually be spent in an intimate relationship with another person. We do not believe this. We believe that much more intimate sharing is available between people than they usually experience.

In the office, an intimate conversation might be very short. A co-worker might say to you, "I'm so discouraged," and you might reply, in full truthfulness, "I am too." Or, you might say, "Gee, I feel so great! Linda and I hit it off! We're going to get married in two months!" Your office partner might respond: "Great! Congratulations! I like you, and I like her, and I believe you'll have lots of fun together."

In these samples, notice the absence of put-downs. Do notice the openness. Note that intimate ways of spending time do not have to include sex. The strokes we receive unconditionally for our Natural Child are ones we almost always get and thrive on during intimacy.

Notice also that we do not have to reveal deeply private parts of our personal life in order to spend time intimately with someone else. What is necessary is that we do not spend time in any of the other ways we have listed in order to avoid intimacy. Most importantly, it is crucial that both people feel open, free, and trusting. (Some people in TA believe that one person may be intimate while another may treat the time spent as an activity or a game.) Intimacy invites intimacy from the other person, whether it be simply "straight talk" between two co-workers or deep intimacy between two good friends.

In Chapter 8 we shall show you more ways to feel OK yourself and to get others to join you in OK feelings and activities.

SUMMARY

We all have to decide how to spend our time; it is a decision we cannot avoid. We spend it in one of six ways. Efficient use of time results in work getting done, good feelings, and a pleasant environment in which to work and make friends. Inefficient time use—most particularly in games—results in bad feelings, inefficiency, destructiveness to persons and perhaps property. You can learn to detect games and stop them rather than allowing yourself to be hooked into them. When you do not detect them in time to avoid them, you can still avoid bad feelings and minimize them in the future.

SUGGESTED ACTIVITIES

1. Estimate the percent of your time at work that you spend in the following categories:

Withdrawal   Activities   Ritual   Pastimes   Games   Intimacy
_____   _____   _____   _____   _____   _____

Now estimate the percent of your time spent in each of the following categories on a three-day holiday from work:

Withdrawal   Activities   Ritual   Pastimes   Games   Intimacy

—————— —————— —————— —————— —————— ——————

For the sake of greater efficiency and pleasure, do you need to change the ways in which you invest your time? If so, how?

2. Some people have been trained to accomplish and achieve. They work well; they are often good at whatever they undertake. They are frequently skilled in sports. Yet they often say they are not comfortable with "small talk" (pastiming). How would such people gain from mastering the art of pastiming comfortably?

3. When we ask why a certain procedure is done the way it is, the answer may be, "It's just always been done that way." In such cases, we check to see if the procedure has become ritualized.

   a) List some procedures in your department which seem almost automatic.

   b) What are the reasons for doing them the same way now?

   c) Look at them as if you were an outsider who knows nothing about such procedures.

   d) Consider alternate methods to accomplish the same or similar goals.

   e) Is there a better way to do them?

4. a) Remember a recent work experience that you left with bad feelings.

   b) Which ego state were you in? If you wanted to criticize or help, you were almost certainly in your Parent state. If you felt embarrassed, angry, or scared, you were probably in your Child ego state.

c) Fill in the first three moves of your experience on the model below. Who made the first move? From which ego state? How were the next two responses made?

d) Now chart the cross-up—where the transactions were crossed and the bad feelings were recognized.

e) What other options did you have? If you had responded from another ego state, what would have been different?

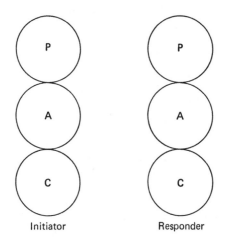

Initiator   Responder

5. All of us play games from time to time. Each of us tends to have our "favorite" game. We tend to repeatedly end up as Rescuer, Persecutor, or Victim. What is your blind spot, the way you allow yourself to become hooked into games? Does this ego state get enough strokes? If not, what will you need to do to remedy the situation?

5

Our Psychological Oxygen

STROKES

Just as ego states are the backbone of TA, so are strokes its
heartbeat. We get our psychological oxygen from strokes.
When we use the word *stroke* in this context, we are talking
about the simplest unit of recognition. When the boss puts her
hand on your shoulder and says, "That was really well done!"
she is giving you a stroke. When you tell Jim you are glad
that you can always rely on him, you give him a stroke.

We first learned about strokes in infancy when our parents
literally stroked our skin. Skin contact remains a very powerful
stroke throughout our lives. A handshake or a pat on the back
may convey far more than words alone.

We all need strokes in order to survive and are all taught
which strokes are valuable and desirable. After we have
learned these lessons, we find ways to get our quota of
strokes. Let's say that you have usually rewarded Mary's work
with compliments. Now she hands you another piece of care-
fully completed work. If you do not give the usual compliments, Mary may wonder what's wrong. On the other hand, if

you return from a two-week vacation and Mary greets you
with only her cheerful daily, "Good morning," instead of,
"How was your vacation? Did you have fun? What did you
see?" then you are apt to feel that something is wrong in the
relationship between you and Mary.

We think of strokes as being positive or negative, conditional
or unconditional. Positive strokes are those that help most
people to feel good. They tell the other person, "You're OK."
Negative strokes are those that would hurt most people, e.g.,
"Charley, you didn't say what I asked you to say in that letter,
and now we are really in trouble." Negative strokes say,
"You're not OK."

Conditional strokes are ones given if the individual behaves in
the way desired by the stroke giver—e.g., "That's a good job
you did on that casting." Unconditional strokes have the greatest stroke value, for they are given simply because you are
you, not because of your behavior—e.g., "I like you"; "I like
having you in this department"; "I like being married to you."

When a person's stroke quota is not met in the accustomed
ways, his or her behavior begins to change. Managers may
spot such evidence as decreased efficiency, tardiness, or increased irritability in their subordinates as indicating these people are not getting the strokes they like on the job. Does this
mean that the manager is to become Big Mama or a psychotherapist? Not at all.

Good managers know when their people change, when things
are not going well for them on the job. They always do *something* with such knowledge. They may choose to discount the
problem and treat it as though it doesn't exist. For minor dis-
turbances, this may work; the person may "snap out of it" and
take care of the problems without help. Or, the manager
might show interest by seeking out and spending some time

with the troubled subordinate. In so doing, the manager is stroking that employee.

Each of us has our own quota for strokes. Some of us need only a few strokes from others; others need many. Remember when you were promoted from the ranks to the job of manager? You probably felt different when you were with your former associates. One of the big differences is that you got fewer Child-to-Child strokes when you became manager. And you probably gave fewer strokes to their Child ego states also. As manager, you may have already learned that the person near the top of the ladder gets few strokes from those below. You may need to find another basis for exchanging strokes.

Changes in stroking patterns become obvious when people move from one job to another. They have been accustomed to some strokes for each ego state in the old job and, on the new job, must find ways to get similar strokes from new people. This becomes glaringly obvious in a situation such as this: Susan had a manager who complimented her on her efficiency and initiative (strokes for her Adult ego state). When she moved to another city to take a new job, the new manager complimented her only on how well she dressed, her pleasant voice, and attractiveness (strokes for her Child ego state). As a result, she has a deficit of strokes for her Adult ego state. Very likely, she will try to teach the new manager that she prefers to get strokes for her Child while off the job and that she wants Adult strokes while at work. The manager has to learn "different strokes for different folks."

TRADING STAMPS

Some folks "save" strokes. How? They save them by converting them, figuratively speaking, into trading stamps. Like the trading stamps we receive in grocery stores and filling stations, these stamps are regarded as valuable.

The person who saves positive strokes will save them in the form of gold stamps. After saving enough books of gold stamps, for example, Mary might feel: "Okay, I've got enough gold stamps. I can now trade them in on a free dress (car, vacation, etc.)". In this case "free" means free from guilt. It is as though the person has said, "I've got enough earned. I've worked hard and long. I don't need to feel guilty if I go on a vacation." Yes, she could have taken her vacation when it was time or when she felt tired and stale. However, if she is a gold-stamp saver, she will feel that she must save enough gold stamps in the form of saved units of recognition, appreciation, or praise before she can go on vacation guilt-free.

The person who saves negative strokes saves them in what have been called brown stamps. Each of these stamps represents an incident in which the individual feels he or she has been "dumped on," cheated, kicked, disregarded, etc. For a few books of brown stamps, Fred may feel entitled to a free rage, a free drunk, a free "I'll call them up on Monday and say I'm sick. They've dumped on me enough already." If he has saved up a big store of such stamps, he may feel entitled to a (guilt) free theft from the company, industrial sabotage, free divorce, etc.

Why would anybody want to collect brown stamps? Remember, we said that everybody needs strokes. If the person survives infancy, we assume he or she has gotten at least a minimum amount of positive strokes. After this, if the individual doesn't get positive strokes, he or she will find ways to get negative strokes. Perhaps the best way the person can find to be noticed is to "goof up," get teachers or parents or bosses mad, agree to do a job and then neglect to do it. In a word: If the person can't get positive strokes, he or she will take negative. When the manager tries to give such a person a positive stroke, the person distorts it into a negative stroke. This is particularly evident in "hard" games of "Kick Me." In these, the individual manages to get kicked—figuratively or literally—repeatedly, and stores them up as brown stamps. When you are confronted with such an individual, you don't have to provide the kick—if you refuse to deliver it, the individual will find someone else to play the game.

Some managers have spent a lot of time in trying to persuade an individual that his or her collection of brown stamps is worthless. We recommend that managers recognize brown-stamp collectors early in order to avoid this time waste. If the person consistently gets negative evaluations, plays the game of "Kick Me," and does not respond to interest and praise (gold stamps), then he or she is probably a brown-stamp collector. Curing a brown-stamp collector is not a job for a manager. We do not know any approach to management science which can correctly claim on-the-job cures for such individuals in ordinary work situations.

SWEATSHIRTS

We are tempted to say: "By their strokes, you will know them." Some people are so easy to spot according to their favorite type of strokes that we think of them as wearing a sweatshirt with a logo proclaiming how they like to be treated. Such a sweatshirt also tells how the individual likes to structure time.

Remember the last time you asked someone to do a certain job for you and were met with some whined excuses? It takes no great stretch of the imagination to picture that person wearing a psychological sweatshirt emblazoned with: "I can't." The perfectionistic boss can readily be envisioned as wearing a sweatshirt which says in front: "I demand perfection." However, look at the back side and you may imagine the statement: "I knew *you* would not be perfect." Managers are familiar with the person whose sweatshirt says on the front, "Help me," and on the back says, "I knew you couldn't."

If you think of people as wearing psychological sweatshirts and practice your skills at reading their sweatshirt messages, both front and back, you will be able to predict many of the ways in which these people spend their time and also their characteristic games and rackets.

Front	*Back*
I'm really kinda dumb. . .	But I'm smarter than you are!
I'm helpless. . .	I knew *you* couldn't help!
I'm sexy. . .	But don't come close!
I work hard. . .	You're lazy!
I just love to help others. . .	You poor helpless slob.

RACKETS

What's a racket? Remember someone you've known who is usually angry or sad or helpless, or who has some other habitual unpleasant feeling. If they have bad feelings and find what to do about them from their Adult ego state, they are not in a racket. If, however, they permit these nonproductive feelings to prevail, then we say that they are in a racket. For instance, how did Jack, an angrily NIGYYSOBing boss, get that way? He almost certainly learned in his original family that when the going got rough, the thing to do was not to show fear or sadness; he learned that he should get angry. Jack's family taught him, no doubt, that anger was a somewhat "sacred" feeling. When he got angry, things happened. People may have let him alone, may have stopped asking him for anything, or may have treated him like a little Caesar. Many people initially develop into little dictators because of their families' response to their rackets. The term racket aptly describes these repetitive nonproductive feelings because they function like extortion rackets. With an individual in an anger or sadness racket, other people give what the racketeer wants—to be left alone, to be boss, etc. Those who "give" to the racketeer often feel as victimized as did victims of old-fashioned extortion rackets. Rackets hide authentic feelings. In the example above, Jack learned so well not to show his true feelings that now he no longer knows what they are. He only knows and shows the cover-up feeling. Emotional racketeers often seem to have "overdone" emotional reactions. They may seem only angry, only sad, only helpless. Most on-the-job efforts to show them their genuine feelings will fail.

HOW DO YOU USE YOUR KNOWLEDGE OF STROKES, STAMPS, SWEATSHIRTS, AND RACKETS?

If you think of the idea of sweatshirts, you will soon learn to spot certain individuals as liking to spend time in their rackets. You may then predict which types of games these people are likely to play. You will know in advance that when the game is over, the racketeer will "turn on" his or her favorite bad feeling at the payoff of the game, and you may then know which games to especially avoid. You may also know in advance what the person's "favorite" bad feeling is and plan your strategy accordingly.

With Jack, the NIGYYSOBing boss mentioned previously, you could imagine that he wears a sweatshirt which says on the front: "I demand perfection." On the back, it might read: "AHA! I knew you couldn't do it right!" You could predict that his favorite feeling is anger and that he will look for excuses to indulge this feeling. Knowing that he is a stickler, you would make your reports to him precise and foolproof. If he were worried and under pressure, you would predict that he would be angry. You would know that he spends much time in his Critical Parent. You could engage him in the pastime, "Ain't it awful nowadays about what they give us to work with?"

Suppose someone new in your department wears a sweatshirt that says on the front: "I'm helpless." On the back, it says: "You can't help either." If this person plays a hard "Helpless" game, he or she needs more help than a manager can provide. If the person only whined helplessness occasionally, you would not try to become the Rescuer. You know that would fail. When the newcomer shows helplessness, you would engage that person's Adult ego state by saying something like, "I know it seems impossible, doesn't it? Let's see what options we have. What ways can we make it work?"

We do *not*, of course, expect you to tackle the job of a psychiatrist or a psychologist. As a matter of fact, we believe you should never say to anyone:

1. "You're playing a game."

2. "You're in your Child/Parent/Adult."

3. "You hooked my Child!"

4. "You make me so mad."

No one has only good feelings. There are some days when we feel "down" and some days when we feel "uptight." Perhaps we're tired, worried, sleepy. We can also check to see if our Critical Parent is beating on us, driving us unreasonably. On such days, we are most likely to be involved in transactions that end up with our feeling bad. A most-important principle should be remembered at such times: When you end up feeling bad, *don't take the bad feelings.* This may sound crazy, but you *can* do something instead of sitting there feeling bad. Go to your own Adult ego state. What are the facts? How did you get "hooked?" In which of your ego states? How do you feel?

A simple check list of the major emotions we use follows:

Love	Grief
Anger	Joy
Fear	Sex

Check down this list yourself. Remember what your parents said and showed you about the expressions of each of these major feelings. Most of you will find that at least one of them was somewhat taboo in your original family; you were not supposed to express that feeling as freely as some of the others.

How do you feel when things don't go right at work? What is the bad feeling you have most often? Anger? Sadness? Despair? If you are not sure, make a chart so you can answer this question more accurately. Most of us have a "favorite" bad feeling, one we express over and over. How do you express this bad feeling? Productively? If so, great! If not, check out the other feelings that were available to you. Would it be safe and proper to express them on the job? If so, try expressing them—safely. Do you find a different outcome? You may find that the previously unexpressed feeling works even better than the one you've used more often. However, there will still be times when you feel angry, sad, or some other unpleasant feeling. Not all bad feelings are rackets. Only the repetitive, nonproductive ones are rackets.

THE DRAMA TRIANGLE

One of the most useful concepts in transactional analysis is the drama triangle, first discovered by Dr. Stephen Karpman and illustrated here in Fig. 27. Any game may be diagrammed on this triangle and it presents some of the most-important clues for analyzing games. All games involve a "switch." Let's illustrate the switches in a game of "I'm Only Trying To Help You." Terry, on a coffee break, says to Dana and Dale, "I don't know what to do about this memo I got from my manager. The memo sounds like it's trying to say two things at once." The words sound almost innocent and Terry's facial expression reflects worry. His voice is a helpless whine. Terry is thus presented as Victim. Dana and Dale offer help. They guess at the manager's motives; they recall previous unclear memos from this same manager and how they were finally interpreted. Their every suggestion of help (in this case, Rescue) is ignored or Terry tells them why it won't work. As they become frustrated, Terry sees this. He smiles briefly and faintly while saying, "We can't figure it out here. I'll just go ask the manager what it all means." Dale and Dana are frustrated. They tried to help. Terry had not asked for help except by the ulterior transaction of the helpless look and voice. Whereas Terry presented as Victim and they as Rescuers, Terry ends up Persecutor (they couldn't help enough) and they as Victims.

The drama triangle

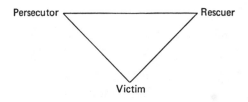

Fig. 27 The drama triangle

In genuine helping, no bad feelings result. In games of help-ing, bad feelings do result. Does this mean that when your help is not appreciated and you feel bad that you have been playing a helping game? Probably so.

When this happens, think back. Did the person present as a Victim? If so, how was this done? Did the person *ask* for help? "I don't know what to do about this problem," is not a request for help. It is a statement (usually crooked at that). The person may think that a "straight" request for help has been made. Next time you hear such a person seemingly asking for help, you might ask, "What have you tried? What options are there? What will happen if you do this or do that?" If the person pre-sents as a Critical Parent Persecutor, you might ask for facts and concrete suggestions as to how the job could be done better. Until you practice, you'll probably miss more transac-tions in which people present themselves as Rescuers. They seem to be the "good guys" until you suddenly become aware that you are being given much more help than you ever wanted. In summary, one of the quickest ways out of the drama triangle is to go to your Adult and ask, "What are the facts?" With more skill, you might decide to optionally engage the other person's Natural Child or Nurturing Parent.

DISCOUNTS

Discounts are defined as "nonrelevant" transactions. As a generator of bad feelings, they cannot be surpassed.

In early childhood, children gather discounts galore. Little Suzy, age three, walks into her parents' bedroom, clutching her blanket and sobbing softly.

Mother: "What's the matter, Suzy?"

Suzy: "I'm afraid. There's something over in the corner of my room."

Mother: "Don't be a silly goose, Suzy. There's nothing there to be afraid of—now you go back to bed and go to sleep."

Suzy said she was afraid. Mother said nothing about Suzy's fear. Her response was not relevant to the youngster's fear. Therefore, we say mother discounted the fear by acting like she had not heard anything about it. If this is repeated often enough by parents, Suzy may grow up with enough Critical Parent "tapes" that she actually discounts her own feelings and perceptions, giving rise to self-discounts.

Discounting Others

In organizational work, individuals discount by ignoring (not responding) or "putting down" other peoples' ideas or contributions. In a team project or partnership, the making of significant decisions without the presence of some of the members of a group is a form of discounting those persons.

If Sheila shows no consideration for the feelings and preferences of her subordinates, she will usually discount them. The message they receive from her, even though she doesn't say it out loud, is, "You are not important." One of the choices that the subordinates have is to begin to discount Sheila except when they must deal with her. There are ways for subordinates to discount the boss and this results in a painful situation for the boss or manager. The manager may respond by becoming more dictatorial; the subordinates may escalate. Soon, a civil war is raging within that department. Such wars lead to psychological games, decreased efficiency, lowered morale, and perhaps even industrial sabotage.

Managers discount subordinates and associates when they indulge themselves in any of the following common Parent-type behaviors:

... make unilateral decisions without consulting those who will be affected by the decisions;

... overexplain fairly obvious situations as if the other person were incapable of understanding the problem without elaborate details;

... describe extensively every detail of a procedure, even after the other person has performed the task satisfactorily at a previous time;

... ignore most feelings and needs of associates and subordinates;

... overdemand attention, even praise, in order to satisfy excessive egocentric needs;

... don't listen to the other person or don't respond relevantly to points made by the other person;

... exhibit a condescending manner or give other people "crooked" strokes (strokes that are not genuine, but calculated to manipulate the other person into agreement);

... use big words, foreign phrases, drop names of well-known people, prefer gobbledegook to clear English, in order to move the other person into a putdown, or "underdog," position, so the discounter thinks he or she is putting himself or herself into the "topdog" position.

Self-discounts

Self-discounters operate from a basic "I'm not OK" position. They have enough not-OK Critical Parent tapes to continually beat down their Child ego state into a not-OK posture most of the time. The inferiority feelings generate a self-concept that is best described by the following answers to the "Who Am I?" question.

... I don't have very good ideas compared to the rest of the staff here.

... People are not really interested in what I might have to say.

... The best way to keep out of trouble is to keep my mouth shut and *never* volunteer.

... I wish I could express myself better.

... I can't take on responsibility like others seem to be able to do around here.

... If I don't try, I can't fail.

Closely allied to self-discounts is the belief that others "make me" think, feel, or act in a certain way. "He makes me so mad" is a typical statement by a person who has not yet developed sufficient awareness and stamina to assume full control over his or her own thoughts, feelings, and behaviors. In the early stages of learning to use TA, you may be tempted to tell someone, "You hooked my Child." The more-accurate statement is, "I let you hook my Child." This way, you keep tuned in to the fact that you are in control of which ego state you respond from. Many people don't like this responsibility; they prefer to believe that others can *make* them feel bad. Of course, someone can make us feel bad if they punch us in the nose, but once we know we have choices of which ego state to use in our response, they no longer have the power to make us feel bad by what they say.

SUMMARY

Everyone needs strokes for each ego state. A deficit of accustomed strokes leads to changed attitudes and performances. Managers can easily notice the preferred stroke patterns of individuals and, without becoming psychologists, can usually see that reasonable stroke needs are met on the job.

Brown-stamp savers invite others to give them more brown stamps until the whole organizational climate becomes unproductive.

People who habitually Rescue others often end up as Victims.

People often try to accommodate emotional racketeers by compliance. For example, a person with an anger racket may extort compliance. Such a response may keep the peace briefly; in the long run, it does not.

Executives who repeatedly discount people or problems create major organizational catastrophe and personnel turnover.

Discounting of oneself may be one of the greatest organizational hazards of all. On the surface, such people seem compliant, even helpless. They save stamps from bad feelings, leading to depression and decreased efficiency. They also may strike back, as by embezzling.

Managers are not going to cure self-discounters or those who collect huge amounts of brown stamps. They can learn to recognize such people quickly and discharge them if possible. If not, put them in places where they are not likely to hurt themselves or the company.

SUGGESTED ACTIVITIES

Strokes

1. a) How do you and your most-valuable employee greet each other each day?
   b) How do you greet each other when you have been away on vacation?
   c) How can you tell when this person is not his or her natural "old" self?
   d) What do you do then? What kind of strokes do you give her or him?

2. a) *Each ego state needs strokes.*
   b) At work, do you get adequate strokes for your Parent by helping, teaching, coaching, leading?
   c) Do you get adequate Adult strokes for knowing as much as you do, being as skillful as you are?
   d) Does the Child in you get enough recognition for being a good person? Fun to be with? Creative?

3. If the answers to any of the questions in item 2 are *no*, then ask yourself:

   a) Is the job the place to get the strokes I am missing?
   b) If so, what behavior must I change in order to get them?
   c) If the job isn't the place, what will I have to do differently away from work in order to get them? (Many managers receive adequate recognition for their Parent and Adult

states on the job. They may need to change some off-
the-job behavior in order to get their Child needs met.)

Stamps

For this activity, we recommend that you take a separate
sheet of paper and read the following, pausing to answer as
you go. Remember a recent situation that ended with your
feeling sad, mad, cheated, or some other unpleasant feeling.
Write it down on the sheet. Now, are you willing to tear up
the sheet and forever put away that bad feeling? Or do you
still feel there is something unfinished about the situation? Are
you still saying to yourself, If only I had said_____? or
done_____? Write down the name of your bad feeling
(sad, mad, etc.).

How did you learn what to do with this bad feeling when you
were younger? What did your parents *tell* you to do when you
felt this way? What did your parents themselves *do* when they
felt this way?

Would you accomplish anything useful by reopening the situation? (Use your fact-finding Adult for this.)

If so, what is the best way to accomplish this so that you and
the other party can both win something?

If reopening it would not be useful, will you now tear up and
forever discard this collection of brown stamps and never
again feel bad about the incident?

Rackets

1. Think of someone in your department who seems more
   angry, more sad, more helpless than you believe is indicated. What feelings does this person *not* show as much as

you would expect? If this person shows more helpless behavior than you would expect, does he or she show anger as much as you would expect? If so, would it be safe to say, "After this incident, you seemed to feel that the whole situation was hopeless. Is that the way you felt? I believe I'd have felt angry if I'd been involved in it. Were you?"

2. The word emotion originally meant *moving away from.* Feelings show up in behaviors. There is no way we can *not* communicate with others. They will know something about how we *feel* from what we *do.* Look at what your early teachers taught you, first by behavior and later by words. On the list below, fill in what each parent did and said to express the feelings listed. What do you do now to express these feelings? Were any of them taboo in your original family? Do you choose not to express these emotions because better judgment says you should not? Or are you still listening to old Parent tapes that may no longer be applicable?

Feeling	Mother		Father		You
	Did	Said	Did	Said	Do
Love					
Anger					
Fear					
Grief					
Joy					
Sex					

Discounts

How good are you at helping a self-discounting employee? If, for instance, someone says, "I couldn't possibly do that," what do you do? Accept the statement at face value and give up? Assist the employee to grow in abilities and confidence? If you try to help and the employee continues to act helpless and you begin to feel annoyed, you are likely to be playing a "helping" game. If so, do you try harder? Give up? Rage? Avoid bad feelings by learning how helpless games proceed and stop them sooner next time? (Remember: not all helping is a game.)

6

You've Got to Motivate Them

One of the most pervasive problems for managers of every level is the question of how to motivate subordinates. The motivational theories offered in most management training programs are too numerous to describe, but the most-often encountered seem to be derived from either the "Theory X-Theory Y" explanation or the "motivator-hygiene" theory. Our aim in this chapter is to show how transactional analysis can serve to implement the actualization of theory into practice by suggesting specific transactional operations within the elements important to each of those major theories. Additionally, we will relate some basics of information theory to applications of TA in order to improve communication effectiveness, both written and oral.

THEORY X-THEORY Y

Dr. Douglas McGregor, a professor of management at the Massachusetts Institute of Technology, was one of-the first to associate a management "style" with an individual's belief or value system. One cluster of beliefs about enterprise, management, and people was labeled by Dr. McGregor simply as "Theory X" and included the following:

1. Management has the responsibility for organizing and controlling the productive elements of an enterprise—people, materials, machinery, and money.

2. The "people" element requires that management motivate, direct, control, and otherwise modify people's behavior to satisfy the needs of the organization.

3. If "management" didn't intervene, people would be apathetic, resistant, or even hostile to the needs of the organization.

4. The typical person is:
   a) lazy and dislikes to work;
   b) lacking in aspiration, avoids responsibility and prefers being led to leading;
   c) unresponsive to organizational needs and by nature self-centered;
   d) inherently resistant to change;
   e) naive, not very quick-witted, and easily manipulated by Machiavellian-type managers having superior intelligence and power.

The Theory-X continuum, depicted in Fig. 28, ranges from "weak" (also called "soft") at one end to "strong" (or hard) at the other. The soft approach is termed "permissive" by some, and we can note that the term usually connotes derision when used by Theory-X managers who favor the hard approach. On the other hand, the advocates of a soft Theory X often see the hard approach as coercive and undesirable.

Fig. 28   The Theory-X continuum

Motivation is usually regarded by Theory-X managers as requiring a "carrot and stick" approach, which consists of punishing prohibited behavior and rewarding productive behavior. The punishment is most often in the form of withholding rewards, which are typically conceived of as money, benefits, and working conditions or, in extreme cases, the basic matter of being employed in the organization at all.

A Theory-X organization is one that is managed by those who, in general, embrace a value system and a belief about people and their motivations as described in the list above. It is management by direction and control, whether soft, hard, or firm and fair.

Theory-X organizations and managers have produced Theory-X people, suggests McGregor, because there has been no recognition that higher levels of human needs other than just holding a job, making money, or attaining comfortable working conditions exist. The higher levels of human needs are for meaningful social relationships, ego needs (or the need to have esteem from others and self-esteem), and for realizing one's highest potential. Essentially, people become lazy and avoid responsibilities when (1) they are expected to be lazy and to avoid responsibilities, and (2) the only rewards deal with basic physical and security needs.

McGregor's cluster of assumptions about the enterprise which has been identified with his Theory Y starts out with the same assumption as does Theory X; the differences begin thereafter.

1. Management has the responsibility for organizing and controlling the productive elements of an enterprise—people, materials, machinery and money.

2. People are not inherently passive or resistant to change or unresponsive to organizational needs. They have become so only because of their experience in the organization.

3. The motivation and readiness to put forth effort to achieve organizational goals, to assume responsibility, and to grow and develop are present in practically everyone. Management is responsible for helping people develop these qualities in themselves.

4. The major task of managers is to arrange the organizational environment and operations so people can release their best productive efforts toward achieving organizational goals through initiating their work objectives and directing themselves toward attaining them.

Theory X relies heavily on external control, while the success of Theory Y depends largely on the extent to which people can exercise self-direction and self-control. Considerable energy would have to be expended in an organization for a manager to shift from a Theory X to a Theory Y frame of reference.

One of the problems basic to making such a shift, insofar as the individual manager is concerned, is the extent to which the manager's life position has been basically "I'm OK, You're Not OK." Holding this life position for a period of time leads to distrust of subordinates, to checking up on others, and, if the manager is a gamesplayer, to the game of NIGYYSOB (I'm OK, You're Not OK). The manager tends to attract the *reciprocal* type of individual (I'm not OK, You're OK) as a subordinate and the two life-position patterns are said to *reinforce* each other (Fig. 29).

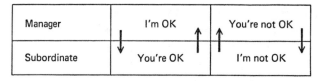

Fig. 29 Two reciprocal, reinforcing life positions

Beyond affording ideal conditions for boss-type NIGYYSOB-ing games, this pattern provides a double-locked-in bind that leads to serious, performance-deteriorating situationᶜ within the organization.

The major question for the manager and the subordinate is: How do we *implement* the implications of Theory Y? How do we turn theory into practice? Transactional analysis contributes at least some of the answers in person-to-person relations and transactions, which in turn powerfully affect the entire organizational climate.

1. The manager, who through awareness and self-contracts can get more frequently into an "I'm OK, You're OK" position, will invite associates to acquire an "I'm OK, You're OK" position likewise. The reciprocal, reinforcing positions lead to increasing mutual trust and encourage both persons to release their energies in productive outlets.

2. Theory Y provides food for thought (for the Adult) and a structure of reality against which a manager can update Parent "tapes." As we have moved from a survival society to a society increasingly concerned with identity (according to Dr. William Glasser), the importance of wages, benefits, and merely having a job as motivators has probably diminished to a point of little effect.

3. Self-analysis by a manager is now possible, using the ego-gram method. If the manager is conscious of "coming on" to subordinates with a heavy Critical Parent, and if further reflection indicates that most of the transactions emanate from the "not OK" Critical Parent, a manager can reasonably predict that he or she will get Theory-X reactions from subordinates.

4. If the manager has practiced manipulation to pressure workers toward greater productivity, the manager has the choice of moving from manipulative to authentic relations with subordinates by adopting authentic third-move responses (Chapter 3).

5. Through stopping discounting of and gamesplaying with others, the manager can stop the great energy drain in counterproductive activities and begin to help others build toward realizing a higher level of their own potentialities.

None of this suggests that managers should give up their responsibilities for organizational results. How to best obtain achievement of both organizational and personal goals is the subject of Chapter 7, in which a total performance-improvement system will be discussed.

MOTIVATOR-HYGIENE THEORY

Dr. Frederick Herzberg carried Theory-Y concepts into a somewhat more-advanced theory of motivation, in which two types of factors that affect workers' behavior are identified—the *motivators* and the *hygiene* factors. The hygiene factors are said to be related to "animal" needs of people and are sometimes called maintenance factors or dissatisfiers; the motivators are said to be related to the "human" needs of people and are sometimes referred to as growth factors or satisfiers. Additionally, the hygiene factors are described as being related primarily to the job environment, while the motivators are related primarily to the content of the job. A summary of the factors is provided in Fig. 30.

Hygiene or Maintenance Factors (Dissatisfiers)	Growth Factors (Motivators/Satisfiers)
Job Environment	Job Content
Company policies and administration	Achievement
Supervision and relations with supervisor	Recognition
Working conditions	Work itself
Interpersonal relations with peers and subordinates	Responsibilities
Money, status, security	Advancement
	Growth and learning

Fig. 30 Hygiene and growth factors

The themes of these two groups of factors point up new and far-reaching learning for management. The themes are these:

■ The *satisfiers*, which lead to improved and increased job performance, *all* relate to the *job* the person does—his or her task, the substance of work, etc. These are called motivators because they lead to changed work behavior in a *positive* direction. These motivators are factors which, when present, tend to install an internal generator in the individual and tend to increase positive attitudes and improved productivity.

■ The *dissatisfiers*, which often lead to diminished quantity and quality of work, *all* relate to the *situation* in which work is done, the environment *not* directly related to the work itself. These are called hygiene or maintenance factors because they are powerless to lead to changed behavior in a positive direction and they only serve to prevent negative job performance.

The Motivators and Transactional Analysis

The motivators or satisfiers of Herzberg's motivation theory may appear at first glance to have primary foundations in job content. But, even more basic, the motivators are tied to the unique human characteristics and abilities to achieve and experience psychological growth. Our central interest, then, is to consider applications of transactional analysis to the implementation of Herzberg job-enrichment concepts. A listing of the motivators and a brief description of the characteristic process involved suggests that the manager has considerable influence and responsibility for the on-the-job realization of the motivators.

1. *Achievement.* This satisfier is said to be present when the individual is arriving at solutions, utilizing his or her highest skills, producing, making a contribution, inventing, developing ideas, meeting objectives, and getting feedback on worthwhile results. The manager of the individual can facilitate realization of this motivator by the following:

■ Transact on the Adult level. Use measures of results in discussing accomplishments of objectives.

■ Provide *training* in decision making, problem solving, and probability estimating. Share with the subordinate how you plan for and manage the department.

■ Avoid too much Nurturing Parent, which will ultimately lead to a rebellious Child—"I'd rather do it myself"—response from the subordinate.

2. *Recognition.* Recognition functions as a motivator when not only the individual realizes he or she is achieving, but management, and perhaps fellow workers, give tangible evidence that they also recognize this. Beyond this recognition for achievement lies the even more-pervasive need for being appreciated as a human being with human aspirations and limitations. The following applications of transactional analysis by the manager may provide a portion of this.

■ Try *un*conditional strokes instead of conditional strokes: "Things go better when you're around—it's good to have you on the team!"

■ Analyze each individual's proclivities toward games playing, stamp collecting, or racketeering. How does the person characteristically get strokes? Is there a tendancy to avoid positive strokes or to distort them into negative strokes?

■ Stroke Parent, Adult, *and* Child levels. Intimacy has been described as the free exchanging of strokes in all three ego states.

3. *Work itself.* This element deals with job content *related to the individual's specific interests* (what's interesting to that person?). Variety is important, especially within the job itself (as contrasted to the individual being rotated through a variety of meaningless jobs). Challenging, but not impossible, goals are said to be important. So, try to:

■ Appeal to the curious, spontaneous "fun" Child. Work can be fun. Ask: "How can we get more fun out of this assignment?"

- Encourage the individual to make "contracts" for goal achievement with you, even though you may not have a formal M.B.O. program.

- Share (the touch of intimacy) the excitement of the "I did it" moment. "What's the use of doing a job well if no one cares and no one shares," or words to that effect, is a pertinent thought expressed in a well-known Broadway show tune.

4. *Responsibility.* Descriptions of this include *having a share of the mission*, freedom to do things one's own way providing one gets the desired results, authority commensurate with responsibility, and increasing levels of responsibilities. These suggest:

- Taper off on both the Critical and Nurturing Parent as the subordinate gets more experienced on the job.

- At the Adult level, ask more questions than you answer. Especially, ask, "What are the alternatives?" as the subordinate begins to propose plans and actions.

- Avoid playing the game of NIGYYSOB. If the individual should fail to achieve the result agreed upon, analyze why. Develop remedial actions *with* the subordinate.

5. *Advancement.* Advancement includes higher-order work assignments, or an increase in complexity of tasks, as well as actual job promotion.

- Avoid the "don't exceed me" ogre or witch messages from your Child.

- Build your capacity to feel pride in your Nurturing Parent as you see a subordinate move up.

- Discuss with the subordinate a definite career-path plan and commit your time, energy, and thought to the implementa-

kind of treatment to expect from you; what your expectations are; what kind of results you want him or her to produce. Actually, the beginnings of *trust* between two people start with increasing the element of *certainty* between those two people. TRUST has two aspects in business, industry, and government: interpersonal and organizational.

1. *Interpersonal.* This type of trust usually results after a high confidence level has been built between two people, which permits openness and honesty. In transactional-analysis terms, openness is the sharing of the self with the other person in three areas:

- *Values*—of the Parent. This involves an exchange of understandings about what you both feel is "right" and what is "wrong," plus *acceptance* of the other person, whatever his or her built-in value system.

  For example: Jane is a supervisor in flight services for a national airline. She is extremely supportive of the need for a strong union for the stewardesses she supervises. Helen is the manager to whom Jane reports. Both have been with the airline for fifteen years and, in fact, started out together in the same training class. Helen grew up in a family holding strong antiunion bias; her father was an executive with one of the larger industries in the country. Jane's father was a coal miner whose brother died in a mine explosion, and he still blames lax management and a weak union for the accident.

  The two women have had long discussions, even arguments, about unions, management, and the workers. Heated as the discussions may get, they are fast friends and maintain an affection and a deep loyalty to each other.

Jane and Helen have learned to share their differences in an open way; they have learned, too, that you don't have to *agree* with another person's values in order to *accept* that person.

■ *Goals and plans*—of the Adult. The planning, probability estimating, data gathering, and data processing is facilitated when there is mutual respect for the other person's technical abilities, intellectual competence, and professionalism. When this respect has been established, the trust level is increased and there is an openness to exploring goals and objectives in a mutual give-and-take climate.

For example: The development of a career plan is one of the requirements of the personnel department of all managers in the plant. George Markham is an assistant manager whose boss, Alvin Smartly, has recently been brought from the outside. When George began to outline his career path in writing, he felt uncomfortable in relying on the new manager for guidance in such a key element in his future progress. The new manager recognized his own deficiency in being able to advise George and arranged for a highly experienced personnel manager to sit in on the development of the plan. The increased confidence on the part of George during the career-plan discussions *after* the experienced man had been brought in was obvious.

■ *Feelings*—of the Child ego states involve trust in three ways. The other person (1) will not say something, or withhold information just to make me feel good, (2) will not go into a Vengeful Child state and intentionally try to harm me, and (3) will tell me about his or her "bad" feelings whenever I am involved in the bad-feeling situation.

2. *Organizational.* Trust within the organization seems to require a network of interpersonal trust situations and, in addi-

tion, a general sharing of organizational values, goals, and feelings (if an organization can be said to have these attributes). Trust is initiated by top management by openness of information. Guarded information, on the other hand, is viewed with suspicion by most employees. Goals should be participatively developed by as many levels of the organization as possible.

Communication: A Network of Understanding

The enabling behavior is two-way communication and the elimination of barriers preventing two-way communications.

1. *Sending.* In transactional-analysis terms, authentic two-way communication must be game-free. Analysis of the transaction to determine crossed and complementary communications, plus recognition of sending ego states and the careful choice of responding ego states, can increase the effectiveness of a manager.

2. *Receiving.* Requires about as much attention to *observing* the nonverbal cues, including kinesics, as *listening* to the actual words and tone. In face-to-face communications, observe especially:

- Facial expressions—including eye movements
- Gestures and movements of parts of the body
- Posture, including tension or lack of tension of muscles.

The Three Components of Meaning in Communications

Three elements of meaning, either implicit or explicit, are *facts*, the *feelings* about those facts, and the *purposes* of the communication. Those who get too engrossed in transactional analysis sometimes miss the importance of one of the essential tasks of communication: to deal effectively with meaning. Let's look at how to do so.

1. *Facts.* It would be easy to say, "Use the Adult ego state when dealing with facts." The question is: "What are the operations involved in 'using the Adult ego state?'" So, we have a more-explicit way to state this: "Use operational terms, definitions, and instructions."

> *Example:* Instead of saying "praise the employee who turns in a better than expected job," we must define operationally what praise is. We have done so in Chapter 7 (see Fig. 31). Facts also need to be expressed in concrete instead of abstract terms. The term "democratic leadership" means little to the individual in a supervisory training program until the kinds of events, interactions, and outcomes are described in concrete detail—words exchanged, the actions observed, the results attained.

Transactional analysis tends to develop its own abstractional jargon. Phrases such as "cathect the Adult" may be tossed about instead of describing the operations involved and the behaviors that provide evidence of the accomplishment of the act.

2. *Feelings.* Feelings are mostly in the Child ego state but may arise in the Parent ego state, and both need to be considered. The precaution in dealing with "facts" is to be aware of the "feeling" ego states that may be elicited, and this element of meaning is the one for which transactional analysis provides the most insight. We now have a method of under-

standing how bad feelings develop and of diagramming the processes by which better feelings may be developed.

3. *Purposes.* Communication theory suggests dealing with purposes explicitly. Transactional analysis's contribution is to understand that an individual's purposes may not always be *goal*-oriented, but may be *game*-oriented. Additionally, the purpose of the communication may be to elicit strokes from the other person, or to reinforce a life position. Finally, this encounter may be only another scene in the life script, or a method of advancing the life script of the individual, without any other specific purpose attached to it.

WRITTEN COMMUNICATIONS

It may seem inappropriate to be concerned with written communications in a book about transactional analysis. Yet much of the analytical technique applied to face-to-face transactions can clarify the outcomes of written communications. Actually, there is a stimulus (sending message) and a response (reaction) of some kind, even though internal, from the reader.

Planning Memos and Letters

We are all familiar with the typical management-to-employee memoranda which adorn the bulletin boards of major corporations and begin with the time-worn phrase, "Effective immediately...," such as the following memo.

TO: All employees

SUBJECT: Employee parking regulations

Effective immediately, all employees

shall use only the parking spaces allocated

to employees at the rear fence line of the

shopping center. Violators will be subject

to disciplinary action.

The Management

The managers whose tasks include writing memos and letters to subordinates should benefit by analyzing the possible effect of such memos before casting them in concrete and shipping them to destinations in the minds of employees. The analysis could well include:

1. In view of my purposes (getting the reader(s) to think, feel or do something), what is the appropriate ego state I want to aim this communication toward? (list first, and possibly second, choices)

2. What, in view of Item 1 objectives, is the most suitable ego state from which I should draft the memo?

3. Since the memo must stand on its own, there being no chance for personal feedback from the receiver at the time it is read, is it fully explanatory. so as to satisfy the Adult ego state of the receiver and provide *certainty*?

4. Have I avoided the "snarl" words, words that are known to elicit a negative or defensive reaction from most people? (For example, using "interrogate" in place of "interview," starting a sentence containing either fact or opinion with the word "obviously," etc.)

5. Have I refrained from stating an opinion of mine as a fact?

6. Is there overuse of the word "I"?

Analyzing Written Communications

In order to apply some of your knowledge of transactional analysis and communication concepts, study the sample letter provided on p. 110 and answer the following questions:

1. What is your overall impression of the writer, based solely on the letter?

2. From which ego state is the sending message originating?

3. What needs are being expressed by Burton?

4. What ego state of the receiver is most likely to be tapped into by the letter?

5. If Bill Johnson saw the letter, what is the ego state from which he most likely would respond?

6. What would be the effect of this letter on teamwork effectiveness of the officer group in XYZ Corporation?

7. What other options did Burton have in writing this letter?

April 29, 1977

Mr. John Doe, Vice President
ABC Corporation
1101 20th Street
Anywhere, USA

Dear Mr. Doe:

I am mighty sorry that I did not have a
chance to visit with you when you dropped
in at our meeting at the Hilton Hotel last
week. Bill Johnson, our Vice President in
charge of Customer Relations, told me after
my return that he had suggested you drop by.
I'm embarrassed that I was not alerted and
therefore did not get to visit with you
personally.

I realize you were rushed, but I hope you
gained some firsthand impression of our
services and product lines. In any event,
I appreciate your taking time to look in--
and if there's anything further I can do
personally to keep you posted on our
services, I hope you will let me know.

Cordially,

Richard Burton
President

XYZ CORPORATION

SUMMARY

Managers and management theorists have long been concerned with the subject of motivation. The central question seems to be: "How can I get workers and managers to *want* to and actually produce more?" The answer increasingly seems to be: "You don't; they have to want to from the 'inside'; it is not a matter of a person, or an organization, imposing it on people from the 'outside.' "

The Theory X-Theory Y approach suggests that people innately have potential for development, a capacity for assuming responsibility, and readiness to direct their own behavior toward constructive ends. In a sense, people are innately princes and princesses. Unfortunately, organizations and the managers in them have, through manipulation, direction, and control, discouraged the human potential from being expressed. Some organizations have turned the princes and princesses into frogs. Some transactional-analysis concepts may have value in turning around the traditional view of human beings as workers, in improving the interactions between manager and worker, and in upgrading the performance of the entire team. More specifically, the concepts may help to develop an awareness in managers holding a "You're Not OK" life position that their own view of others may lead to continuing deteriorating performance in subordinates who begin to believe they really are *not* OK.

The motivator-hygiene theory of Dr. Herzberg goes a step further to more precisely define the elements of work which lead to "turned-on" performance and results. The problem with the motivators, which are said to have reasonably good probability of "installing an internal generator" in a person, is that they are so difficult for the average manager to understand and to intentionally provide for each subordinate. The active definition of each motivator, or satisfier, was presented in this chapter with "how to" steps for applying them interpersonally with each worker.

A large part of motivation is dependent on manager-subordinate communications. People can easily be "demotivated" by the kinds of communications exchanged between management and workers. The bad-feeling diversion of energy into anxiety, worry, hostility, and depression can be averted to a considerable degree by applying communication concepts, implemented by transactional-analysis guidelines.

Certainty growing out of effective communications will not only provide better performance results because activity is more firmly based in reality, but will also escalate interpersonal trust and openness. Semanticists, the scientists who deal with meaning through communications, have provided tools for dealing more effectively with the three components of meaning—facts, feelings, and purposes—although transactional analysis has most relevant applications to the feelings element.

Written communications can create as many problems as they solve. When the written communication is seen as a transaction and the planning of the communication takes into consideration the possible responses of the receivers, the analysis applied to one-on-one, face-to-face transactions will be equally helpful in improving memos, letters, and bulletins.

SUGGESTED ACTIVITIES

1. Review the description of the typical worker according to Theory X on page 92. Do you have someone working for you who seems to fit that description? Possibly, he or she has come to be that way because of the work environment

(or climate) or because of the way supervisors have treated him or her. What ego state are you in when you judge the behavior of this person to fit the Theory-X description of workers? What can be done to help this person get more satisfaction out of the work situation? In which ego state can you do the best job of planning to help the person?

2. Review the Herzberg motivators (pages 98 through 101). Select someone who reports to you who is performing unsatisfactorily and answer the following questions: Are one or more of the Herzberg motivators of greater-than-ordinary importance to that person? If so, are any of these elements missing from work the person performs? Can you arrange for some of the missing factors important to that person to be added to the work situation?

3. Review several recent communications you have written. Apply the questions on pages 108–109 to one or more of your memos or letters. Could the recipient(s) have been "turned off" by your approach? Left hanging, or uncertain, about any facts you hoped to transmit? Made suspicious of your purposes? If so, try to rewrite the communication to eliminate "static." Decide from which ego state you could most effectively express yourself and to which ego state(s) you should address the communication for best results.

4. Can you discuss your feelings about events in the organization openly with your boss? With your associates? With your subordinates? If not, why not? List the number of discussions of this kind in the past month and with whom. Identify several strong feelings you have experienced in the work situation recently. Were you in your Parent or Child ego states at those times? Which ego states would be best spokesperson for these feelings when you express them to others?

5. Select several subordinates whom you feel you know best and list for each person the tasks you feel are "turn on" tasks, i.e., the job elements that give them the most personal enjoyment and satisfaction as they engage in them. Check with each individual to see what they identify as the "turn on" elements of their work. (These should be the "work itself" motivators.) Have you tuned in to these highly individualized factors accurately? Can you arrange for more of these kinds of tasks to be present in the jobs of those individuals?

7

How'm I Doing and What Do I Do Next?

The two most-often-asked, and frequently unanswered, questions employees direct to their supervisors are: (1) "How'm I Doing?" and (2) "What Do I Do Next?" This applies to all subordinate-manager relationships from the on-line employee up to the top level of management. When these two questions are reasonably well "answered,"* productivity and positive attitudes usually increase; when they are not answered very well, performance seems to deteriorate. Much of the give-and-take between supervisor and subordinate about these two questions is in crossed transactions. Some can be classed as a NIGYYSOB game.

PERFORMANCE REVIEW

The key problem seems to be with the performance-review discussion which, if improperly conducted, can undo in one

---

*"Answered" is used here differently from the usual sense of the word; it implies a two-way discussion with inputs from both manager and subordinate in arriving at an "answer."

hour a good manager-employee relationship that has taken months, even years, to build. Theoretically, if manager and subordinate have thoroughly discussed the objectives and have mutually developed the expectations of one another, the review of accomplishments should be Adult-to-Adult, performance-centered, and relatively anxiety-free. Realistically, what takes place is frequently the opposite.

Attitudinal Factors

In the first place, the mental set held by each of the two parties to the interview may set the stage for failure. The most-common deficiencies leading to ineffective interviews are:

1. Failure of the manager to accept the subordinate as a human being, a valuable person, *unconditionally*. This does not mean the supervisor needs to accept the other person's value system or behavior. It is basically similar to the Christian concept of God's "grace" and requires a fairly well-established life outlook that others are, by and large, OK. However, the performance of the individual may *not* be OK!

2. Overemphasis on "why" the subordinate did certain things that led to less-than-acceptable results. Reality therapy suggests to teachers, managers, and therapists that such emphasis leads mostly to excuse-giving, rationalizations, and cop-outs.

3. Managers trying to be amateur psychologists by delving into personality traits and using labels such as "bad attitude," "lack of aggressiveness," "inferiority complexes," "too intro-vertive," and other similarly difficult traits to define or mea-

sure. The major reaction by subordinates to such treatment is to become defensive and hostile.

4. Using past deficiences to punish, browbeat, or withhold organizational rewards. For the most part, this "discounts" the employees and convinces them that they really are *not* OK.

5. Erroneous notions about "praise" or "criticism." Studies in business organizations have shown that praise frequently has little positive effect on performance and that criticism often has a negative effect on performance.

The "technique" of praising or criticizing has occupied so much space in managerial publications over the past fifty years that it deserves further analysis.

Praise versus Criticism

The organizational study referred to in point 5 above has been thoroughly reviewed and the negative aspects of both praise and criticism appear to apply to only certain kinds of praise and criticism. New insights into praise/criticism transactions has been provided by TA. These are summarized in Figs. 31 and 32.

Just as any word in the dictionary has more than one meaning, we can understand that there could be a Type 1 praise and a Type 2 praise, each with contrasting *operations* and each with differing impact on the receiver. Let's define Type 1 praise as consisting of those operations that have little effect on the performance of the receiver and Type 2 praise as consisting of operations that *might* have a positive effect on performance (see Fig. 31).

Type 1 praise—has little effect on performance of the receiver.	Type 2 praise—may have a positive effect on performance and build an authentic relationship.
1. Generalized praise—such as, "You're doing a good job, Charlie." This is meaningless and it generally rolls off the back of the individual without effect. It is often seen as a "crooked" stroke.	1. Specific praise—such as, "Charlie, you did a great job handling that unpleasant customer with a complaint this afternoon." This communicates to the receiver that the boss has actually observed or heard about the praised action. It is sometimes an OK-Nurturing-Parent-type evaluation, but can be a celebrating Natural Child.
2. Praise with no further meaning. There is no analysis of why a praised behavior is being commended. This "discounts" the persons being praised by assuming they will respond with higher productivity and better morale merely as a response.	2. Continuing with, "The reason I think it was such a good job is because you acted interested, asked questions, wrote down the facts, asked the customer what she thought we should do to make it right." Analysis of this kind permits the employee to internalize the learning experience, to place it in the Adult repertoire.
3. Praise for expected performance, when it may be questioned. Mable, who always gets in on time and is met one morning with, "Mable, you're sure on time	3. Praise for better than expected results...for coming in over quota...exceeding the target...putting out extra effort.

Type 1 praise—has little effect on performance of the receiver.	Type 2 praise—may have a positive effect on performance and build an authentic relationship.
today, you're doing great," from her boss, may wonder what's really going on.	
4. The "sandwich" system—praise is given first to make the person be receptive to criticism (the real reason for the transaction), which is then followed by another piece of praise, hoping, thereby to encourage the person to "try harder" next time, feel better about the criticism.	4. Praise, when deserved, given by itself is believable; when mixed with critique it is suspect. Authentic relations develop better when people talk "straight." When positive conditional recognition is in order, do so; when critique is deserved, do so. Don't mix the two.
5. Praise perceived by the receiver as given in the nature of a "carrot," mainly to encourage the receiver to work even harder in the future.	5. Praise that is primarily to commend and recognize, and does not seek to put a mortgage on the future.
6. Praise handed out lavishly only when the "brass" or higher-ups are present. Employees soon recognize the boss is trying to impress superiors with what a good human being he or she really is in dealing with subordinates.	6. Praise given when it is deserved, not just on special occasions, when it seems to build the image of the praiser to some third party.

Fig. 31 Ineffective versus effective praise

Type 1 criticism—tends to produce a defensive reaction in the receiver and worsening performance.	Type 2 criticism—a type of constructive criticism that may improve performance.
1. Criticism that involves use of the personal "you," e.g., "You're having too many accidents on the lift truck, Bill. What's the matter with you anyway?" It is almost always seen as a "discount" or put down by the receiver. It comes close to being the "blaming game," and tends to be taken as personally threatening.	1. Criticism using a situational description, e.g., "Bill, we're experiencing an increase in lift-truck accidents. What's going on?" This indicates the manager is open to looking at all the facts leading to the unfavorable result.
2. Criticism that is unanalyzed. The subordinate then tends to rationalize the criticism as a personal opinion of the manager ("discounts" the manager's Adult). Or, the manager is viewed as unable to analyze the problems effectively.	2. Discussion of cause and effect with the unfavorable condition perceived by both as the result of one or more casual factors, one of which might even be the manager!
3. If the situation has been properly assessed, some managers are at a loss to provide coaching necessary for the subordinate to improve. This may be the result of ignorance or lack of competency in deciding on the corrective steps.	3. If steps 1 and 2 above have been properly accomplished, it is important for solutions to be outlined and agreed on. If the subordinate can't do this, the manager must provide, or arrange, for a resource that can develop corrective measures.

Type 1 criticism—tends to produce a defensive reaction in the receiver and worsening performance.	Type 2 criticism—a type of constructive criticism that may improve performance.
4. Critique of an individual in public is not only regarded as humiliating by the subordinate involved, but sometimes even more so by other members of the organization.	4. Individual criticism given in private is usually more acceptable. "Saving face" is almost as important in Western cultures as it is in the Orient.
5. Criticism given *only* in the interests of the boss (to get the boss recognition, promotion, or raise) or the organization (more profit or status in the marketplace). These may all be legitimate interests, but *authentic* relationships are not likely to develop.	5. Criticism given *also*, or even chiefly, in the interests of the employee (to provide greater competencies, future achievements, or a more-secure future with the organization).
6. The manager does all the critiquing which sets the stage for a Parent-Child transaction.	6. The subordinate participates in the critiques, even to the point of taking the lead role in defining the unsatisfactory condition, analyzing causes, and suggesting corrective steps.
7. Criticism used as a part of a NIGYYSOB game or to justify withholding raises or promotions.	7. Game-free and racket-free criticism leading toward candor and intimacy.

Fig. 32 Destructive versus constructive criticism

Likewise, the word "criticism," operationally defined, must have at least two distinct sets of operants, which we shall label criticism Type 1 (which results in defensiveness and deteriorating performance on the part of the receiver) and Type 2 criticism (which might result in improved subsequent performance). If there is such a thing as "constructive criticism," it must consist of Type 2 criticism operations (see Fig. 32).

A major effort should be made to avoid the "Parent-Child" transactions in the boss-subordinate discussions during performance review. The "boss-subordinate" phrase itself leads to nonverbal expressions that support and even extend the "topdog-underdog" conflict. The ego state that seeks to control others may be expressed from either Critical Parent or Nurturing Parent and, in either case, from an OK or Not-OK position.

■ The *Not-OK* Critical Parent does so to put down or discount the other person, and thereby enjoys, even superficially, a superior "topdog" position. The diagram of the seesaw in Fig. 33 illustrates the thinking of a person exerting control over another in order to enhance the boss's self-image.

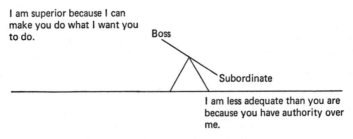

I am superior because I can make you do what I want you to do.

Boss

Subordinate

I am less adequate than you are because you have authority over me.

Fig. 33 Topdog-underdog relation

- The *OK* Critical Parent controls out of firmly held values (regarding the "right" way to do things) with the explanation that the organization, and thus all the people involved in it, will be more likely to succeed and make progress.

- The *Not-OK* Nurturing Parent controls in order to maintain an appearance of being essential to the success of the subordinate, and exemplifies the need to be needed.

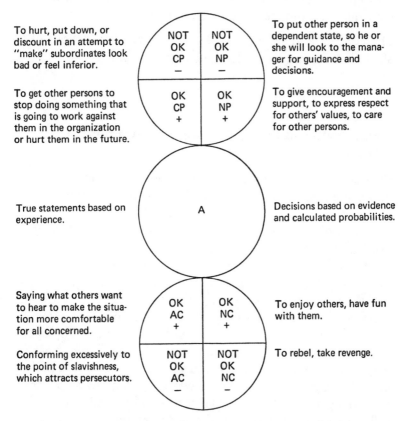

To hurt, put down, or discount in an attempt to "make" subordinates look bad or feel inferior.

NOT OK CP −

To put other person in a dependent state, so he or she will look to the manager for guidance and decisions.

NOT OK NP −

To get other persons to stop doing something that is going to work against them in the organization or hurt them in the future.

OK CP +

To give encouragement and support, to express respect for others' values, to care for other persons.

OK NP +

True statements based on experience.

A

Decisions based on evidence and calculated probabilities.

Saying what others want to hear to make the situation more comfortable for all concerned.

OK AC +

To enjoy others, have fun with them.

OK NC +

Conforming excessively to the point of slavishness, which attracts persecutors.

NOT OK AC −

To rebel, take revenge.

NOT OK NC −

Fig. 34 OK and not-OK sources of strokes and transactions

- The *OK* Nurturing Parent controls out of a genuine and deep concern for the success of the subordinate, giving the individual an opportunity to achieve through incremental learning of skills and know-how.

The most appropriate control behaviors should emanate from the Adult ego state in order for the best manager-subordinate relationships and teamwork to develop. The best kind of manager applies the least amount of control consistent with individual and organizational achievement.

The concept and sources of OK and Not-OK transactions of all kinds is further expanded and illustrated in Fig. 34.

Game Switches during Performance-Appraisal Interviews

One of the disturbing transactions in the performance review, because it is so difficult to analyze, is the "game switch." Before describing one such game switch, let's review the definition of a racket. People are in their rackets when they experience repetitive unpleasant feelings that are counter-productive. The manager who has a "Great Parent" racket must compulsively exhibit goodness and greatness by "doing for" the subordinate as the employee works toward accomplishing established objectives. This hovering is some-times perceived as unwarranted interference by the employee who finally rebels and communicates, "Will you get out of my way and let me do it!" The manager then switches to a plain-tive Child ego state, whining, "I was only trying to help." So, the manager collects a negative stroke and the subordinate collects a bad-feeling payoff of guilt for treating a person with such good intentions so badly. Such a manager may repeat the performance several times a day, experiencing bad feelings and creating nonproductive reactions in both manager and subordinate.

TA TIPS FOR PERFORMANCE INTERVIEWS

By applying transactional-analysis insights to the performance-evaluation interview we can pinpoint major "do's" and "don'ts" for managers and subordinates:

For the Manager:

Do	Don't
1. Ask Adult-oriented questions: "What results did you obtain?" "What did you do to obtain them?"	1. Ask "why" the subordinate did certain things that led to substandard results. It sets the stage for excuse giving or defensive behavior and provides opportunities for "If it weren't for you" games.
2. Commend better-than-expected results—*celebrate* on a Child-to-Child wavelength!	2. Use praise or criticism as a control device to manipulate or extort desired behaviors from subordinates.
3. Use the Critical Parent ego state when you genuinely believe that the subordinate should stop doing certain things that are reducing that individual's effectiveness.	3. Use typical manager games of "NIGYYSOB," "Blemish," or "I'm Only Trying to Help."

Do	Don't
4. Be aware, when discussing steps toward future improvement, of the subordinate moving into a game of "Yes, But."	4. Race around the "drama of life" triangle. It usually starts with you at the Persecutor (Critical Parent) corner; proceeds next to either the Victim or Rescuer corner. In any event, you can usually end up in the Victim position.
5. Use forward-looking Adult questions: "What yet needs to be done to get the result you planned?"	5. Use past deficiencies in performance to prove to employees that they are incompetents.

For the Subordinate:

Do	Don't
1. Move into Natural Child as a relief from Adapted Child—an ego state many subordinates get into during a progress review.	1. Permit yourself to get into resentful, Vengeful Child ego states.
2. Use plenty of facts and evidence, communicating from the Adult ego state.	2. Play victim games such as "Kick Me," "See What You Made Me Do."
3. Ask questions of your manager when you differ about facts or the interpretation of them.	3. Let the interview degenerate into an argument on a "Yak, yak—you are too..."Child-Child transaction.

THE GOAL-SETTING SESSION

Because the performance review is so dependent on the results of the objective-setting session conducted sometime prior to the performance review, it is important to point out some guidelines for more-effective methods of arriving at goals, targets, and objectives. Most research indicates that mutually set goals lead to best accomplishment...IF the subordinate has been accustomed to a participative climate and style of leadership in the manager. The chief roles of the manager and the subordinate are suggested in Fig. 35.

Fig. 35 Roles of manager and subordinate in setting objectives

Subordinate	Manager
Establishes goals and objectives that are challenging. This is as much a "self-contract" for achievement as it is a contract to deliver a result to the boss.	Ascertains that the results sought are attainable but not so easy that they fail to provide a sense of achievement.
Develops yardsticks for measuring results. Operations and interventions must be detailed in order for the results to be accomplished.	Requires that the measures do not cost more to record and report than the result is worth.
Describes steps required to accomplish objectives.	Probes for possibility of better methods being developed by the subordinate.
Develops alternate plans for accomplishing results.	If only one plan is suggested, asks, "What are the alternates?"

Fig. 35 (continued)

Subordinate	Manager
Recommends one alternate plan over the others.	If a specific recommendation is not forthcoming, asks, "What course of action do you suggest?"
Outlines participation required from others if they are not under the control of the individual setting the objectives.	Ascertains from the subordinate how carefully the necessary cooperation has been discussed with those whose cooperation is essential—i.e., how committed they are to provide services.
Describes potential problems that may emerge as objectives are being attained. In TA, the contract for change must include awareness of: "How might you sabotage your own plan?"	Establishes monitoring system and procedure progress checks to assure full awareness of self and subordinates if complications arise.

Of the three phases of a performance-improvement system, the phase of establishing subsequent objectives is most oriented to Adult-Adult transactions. The autonomy of the subordinate is established with the role of the manager shifting largely to that of prober, challenger, and coach. The Parent ego state is occasionally exhibited when discussion turns to "What should we do?" and an exchange of values, standards, and ethics is taking place. But the straight Adult can get dull and boring without some Child-ego-state relief, with specific questions of, "How can we get more fun out of work?" being developed.

DEVELOPMENTAL PLANNING WITH THE SUBORDINATE

The total performance-improvement system guides the interview toward planning for further development of the subordinate. In the total performance-improvement system, it is the job of the manager to guide the interview toward planning for the subordinate's further development. One way that this can be accomplished is by the manager's thinking in response to stimulation from the Nurturing Parent: "How can I help this person to grow in interest and effectiveness on the job?" If you, as manager, direct Nurturing Parent feelings to the subordinate as well as ask Adult questions, you might say something like, "Okay. Now you know that we're pleased you reached the objectives we agreed on. What's the next step forward you'd like to take?" If the subordinate "gets the message" from both Adult and Nurturing Parent states, the answer might be a smile, an obviously pleased feeling, and words like, "I'd really like to move on into sales management someday."

If the manager spoke *entirely* from the Nurturing Parent position, the Natural Child might be pleased. However, the Adapted Child might feel patronized. Balancing the nurturing aspect of the Parent with the realism of the Adult helps keep the planning reasonable and attainable.

The following checklist of items might be discussed with a subordinate in the personal-development portion of the periodic work review and planning session:

1. What are some of the specific tasks you handle on your present job that "turn you on"—i.e., lend zest to the job? (Ask for examples from the past three to six months.)

2. What tasks in previous jobs turned you on that you no longer experience in your present assignment? Describe.

3. Are there any changes you'd like to see brought about in
   . . . this organization?
   . . . your job?
   . . . your relationships with subordinates, associates, me?
   . . . yourself?

4. How will you and I know that the changes have been achieved?

5. What steps can best bring about those changes?

6. Is there a specific kind of work you'd like to be preparing for and moving into at some future time?

7. Do you need help or resources from this organization or me in order to bring about those changes you have discussed, or to prepare yourself for your future ambitions? If so, what?

It is best to have the subordinate write down the objectives for growth and his or her plan to accomplish them, just as with any other management-by-objectives process. Keep in mind that you have an important nurturing role to play in their accomplishment, too. Just as contracts are made between therapist and client in TA, a person may wish to make a contract for growth with himself or herself. A contract is also an appropriate term to use when your commitment is to coach, train, or arrange for specialized training for your subordinate.

ANALYZING PERFORMANCE PROBLEMS

A problem has been defined as "a deviation from a desired standard." Similarly, a performance problem might be defined

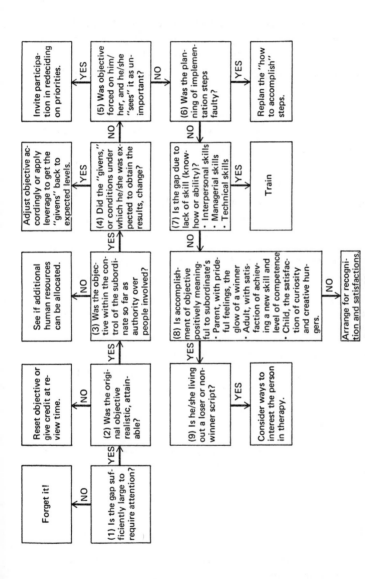

Fig. 36 Analyzing problems of performance. Performance problem analysis begins with a gap between *desired* results and *actual* results. We assume the desired result is important, or it would not have been established in the first place.

as a gap between *desired* (or targeted) results and actual results. The manager who has established reliable progress checkpoints is often faced with the tough task of analyzing both the cause and the correction of the failure to attain desired results.

A psychotherapist must check to be sure that any causal factors of purely physical origin are recognized and being treated medically either before or at the same time as illness of psychic origin is being treated. Similarly, a manager must identify any reasons for the deficiency that are beyond the control of the subordinate charged with the responsibility for an objective *before* beginning to deal with the factors the individual can control.

The "logic chart" in Fig. 36 will help you sort through the factors that are causing the gap. As you eliminate causes of the discrepancy that are not within the complete control of the subordinate, you arrive at two points where TA can be a help in saving the performance problem:

Block 7   If an interpersonal-skills deficiency is causing the less-than-desired results, training in transactional analysis can contribute much to improving the person's skills.

Block 9   If the subordinate is living out a nonwinner or loser script, TA therapy by a qualified clinician may be the first step toward amending the script.

SUMMARY

Many of the cross-ups in communications within organizations are due to ignorance and unawareness of the powerful influence of transactions on communication outcomes.

Complementary, crossed, and ulterior transactions can be diagrammed to better predict what will happen when two people encounter each other.

A total performance-improvement system involves three phases. After the initial goal-setting dialogue has been accomplished, the three phases are:

1. Performance review—looking over past accomplishments.

2. Goal setting—establishing objectives for the coming period.

3. Planning for the growth and development of the individual.

One of the major problems of performance-improvement programming is the misunderstandings that develop during the performance review. These misunderstandings usually grow out of the inability of the manager to properly conduct the interview. Increased use of the Adult ego state by the manager would be evidenced by *analyzing* measurable results in terms of cause and effect. Some Nurturing Parent in the form of the manager's reassurance and personal support for the subordinate in a sometimes trying situation will help. The Critical Parent ego state can be used if the concern is equally in the interests of the individual and the organization, or the manager.

The optimal roles of the manager and the subordinate during the goal-setting phase are when the subordinate "initiates" and the manager challenges, asks questions, and insists on valid back-up data. The dialogue is best accomplished when the two individuals are engaged in Adult planning, probability estimating, and making decisions on plans jointly. The Child ego state can be an important contributor in stimulating creative ideation.

The creation of an individual-development plan with a subordinate requires that considerable energy be invested in the manager's Nurturing Parent ego state. Caution must be exercised to make sure the development plan is achievable within the constraints of organizational realities. This requires "reality testing" by the Adult ego states of both individuals involved in the planning.

Both the manager and the subordinate should be on guard at all times to avoid moving about the corners of the Drama Triangle, from Persecutor to Victim to Rescuer with each playing reciprocal roles at any given instant. It is all too easy for a manager in the Critical Parent to slide into the Persecutor role, while the less-powerful subordinate moves into the Child ego state and assumes the role of Victim.

To prevent inaccurately analyzing substandard performance, we recommend the approach visualized in Fig. 36, the "logic chart." This requires consideration of one factor at a time, with the eventual isolation of the cause of the less-than-acceptable performance, and reduces the chances of ending up with disagreement, impasse, or lose-lose outcomes (where both individuals are losers).

SUGGESTED ACTIVITIES

1. Review a recent performance review that your supervisor conducted with you. How prepared were you for the interview? Allocate what percent of the time you believe you and your supervisor were in each ego state during the interview.

   Remember, if you experienced "feelings" during the interview, you probably had to be in either your Child or Parent ego state.

	Your Boss	You
Critical Parent	___%	___%
Nurturing Parent	___%	___%
Adult	___%	___%
Adapted Child	___%	___%
Natural Child	___%	___%
	100 %	100 %

2. Select a subordinate who is not accomplishing at a satisfactory level. Using the logic chart in Fig. 36, apply the questions until you get at the probable cause of the performance gap. Discuss the situation with the subordinate; invite the individual to review your thinking and your application of logic. If possible, avoid getting into your Parent ego state during the analysis phase.

3. After completing the preceding activity, discuss with the subordinate needed improvements in the "unsatisfactory" performance, based on the needs of the individual and the requirements of the organization. Observe during the discussion the ego state of both you and the subordinate. Which ego state predominates in your case? In the subordinate's case? Does this make for good transactions? Do you think the development plan will be executed? Whose responsibility will it be if it is not?

4. When one of your subordinates merits recognition because of a better-than-targeted result, plan how you will provide the recognition. From which of your ego states would this recognition be most acceptable, given this particular subordinate? Why?

After you have given *recognition*, review the actual effect on the individual. Did he/she seem to be genuinely pleased with it? If not, why not?

5. Think back over the past two or three instances in which you praised an employee. Did you actually (or feel tempted to) take advantage of the situation by adding a request for improving a less-than-satisfactory item in his/her behavior, habits, or performance? Is this wise?

6. In discussing objectives for a subsequent period with a subordinate, what words, phrases, or expressions of yours (either verbal or nonverbal) seem to generate "static" or create resistance on the part of the subordinate to setting worthwhile goals?

8

Transactional Analysis and You

You are often successful at predicting how certain people will live their lives, aren't you? You'll often be right when predicting, "That kid's really going somewhere in life." You may also be right when predicting certain individuals will fail.

How do you do this with such accuracy? We believe that you already have an intuitive knowledge about something we call a *life script*. In the above situations, you made your predictions from knowing that the people involved would lead their lives as though the plans or scripts were already written for them. If you talked with these people, they would probably feel that they had full control over what happened in their lives. Perhaps you've known compulsive gamblers or alcoholics who believed that they had such complete control.

Actually, we believe that all of us live our lives as though the scripts for them were already written. We believe that we got good, healthy messages from our parents and other early caretakers. However, since these people were only human, it is also likely that we got some bad, unhealthy messages from them.

137

Right here we run into some difficulties. In fact, in brief seminars, we give only a very brief introduction to the concept of life scripts. To learn about them is sometimes upsetting, for some people don't like to recognize that even their own parents gave them some messages that were not healthy. Even more uncomfortable to face is the fact that we have done the same to our own children without meaning to harm them in the least. Likewise, we caution our trainees that changing scripts is usually a job for a well-trained therapist, not a manager, friend, or loved one.

Why, then, do we teach them? We teach scripts to help you sharpen your intuitive skills at diagnosing the scripts your associates live, predicting which individuals will be winners, and more quickly spotting losers. Scripts also can help you understand some "failures" you have had with subordinates. Not even the best management skills in the world can change a person's basic life script, for that was decided long before the person joined the work force.

Let's demonstrate with the life plan of the person who works very hard but who doesn't seem to enjoy successes. This individual finally "makes it big"—really does just great—then blows it and loses everything important. That's the pattern over and over. For purposes of illustration, let's say that this is a child whose parents *told* him that he should study hard, work hard, be kind, save money, etc. These directions come from the Parent ego state of both his actual parents. Without going into any of the possible reasons, let's say that he picked up nonverbal signals from the Child ego state of one of his parents—the little kid in the parent—that he should not be any more successful than that Child felt himself or herself to be. This Child state of the parent could let the developing youngster know that he was supposed to study and work hard, be good, etc., but that that wasn't what the Child state wanted.

In fact, this Child may have wanted to be "king of the mountain" and not wanted to be outstripped by the youngster. The smart youngster can eventually feel this and act accordingly.

"If I want to make you happy, I'll have to try hard, but you won't smile. You'll smile and seem happy only if I goof, make mistakes, and don't succeed." Often, we find that one actual parent behaved in such a way that the youngster could imitate a work-hard-but-fail pattern. It seems like "monkey see, monkey do," without either person being aware of the facts. We have illustrated this in Fig. 37.

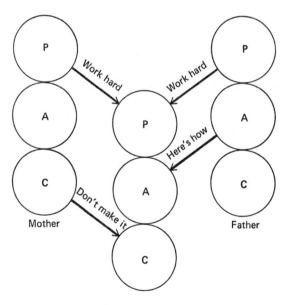

Fig. 37 A "loser" script

So far, we have discussed losers' scripts. There are also winners' scripts. Nobody is 100 percent loser; nobody is 100 percent winner. Our interest is in helping develop your managerial skills so that you may help those who are winners and recognize losers early.

We have heard it said that winners are those people who make good on their own agreements with themselves. Winners have usually gotten Parent messages very similar to those of losers—e.g., study and work hard. The difference lies partially in what they are *shown* about studying and working hard. The main difference, however, is that winners have been liked (most of the time) and encouraged to grow by the Child state of one or both parents.

Winners can be spotted by their track record, of course. Since no one can be 100 percent winner all the time, the record won't be perfect. But many of you can be with someone only a few minutes and still predict with considerable accuracy that a newcomer will be a winner. A large part of this is done with a diagnosis by the Child and Adult ego states in you. You have noted that this person feels, even with faults, that he or she is basically OK. The person also feels that, even with faults, others are OK too.

You would not need many minutes to diagnose a newcomer as a loser if you noted that this person's attitude was "nobody's OK." If the individual's attitude is, "I'm not OK, I don't deserve much, I can't do much good but then neither can you because there's not much hope for anything changing," then you probably won't want to be around such a person very long.

You may have met someone whose attitude was: "Don't confuse me with facts. My mind's made up. I am definitely superior to you. I am very much OK and you are very much not OK. You are my inferior. You'll never please me." Such a person is uncomfortable to be with and we generally are anxious to get away from them. In fact, they may sometimes succeed in helping us feel that perhaps they are right and we are inferior. Most of us have spent some time in the "I'm not OK, you are OK" position—e.g., when we flunk an examination and feel that we should have studied much harder, or when we feel down or depressed. When in this position, we often want to get away from others.

By the same token, when we are with people in the "I'm OK and so are you" position, we "get the show on the road"; we really get things done. When we feel not OK but that others are OK, our tendency is to want to get away. When we let others know that we're OK but they are not, they, in turn, will feel like getting away from us. They'll tend to hide their feelings and even necessary facts from us. If a person feels consistently that nobody's OK, it's time for that person to consider professional help.

A person should also consider professional help if he or she feels consistently not OK, but believes that most other people are OK. This is the position of depression. Depressions always end, but skilled help can help them end sooner, more comfortably, and, above all, more safely. It is primarily depressed people who commit suicide, and the majority of suicides can be prevented by recognizing suicidal tendencies and insisting that the person get skilled professional help. Trying to cheer up the depressed person usually only leads to a more-severe state of depression. Be an expert manager. Leave the treatment of depressions to experts in that field.

THE MINISCRIPT

So far, we have talked about the basic positions the child takes early in life and how these are incorporated into each individual's life script. We have emphasized that each of us learned certain unhealthy and inefficient ways to please the Child in our parents and that to change basic life scripts is usually a job for a trained therapist.

Not-OK Miniscript

As a result of the work of Drs. Taibi Kahler and Hedges Capers, we can now teach you something that you can use on the job to influence how people live their lives: the miniscript. The miniscript concept originated from their observation that the second-by-second behavior of people reinforces their basic life scripts. They believe that each child does indeed receive contradictory messages from its parents, and yet the child is more often aware of ideas picked up from the Parent ego state of its parents than those learned from the Child in the parents. They reduce these messages to only five "drivers." We use their diagram (see Fig. 38) to show that the child learns that if

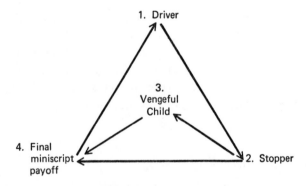

Fig. 38 The not-OK miniscript

it wants to please its parents, it's best to start down the road, compulsively driven to follow the main direction received from actual parents. They believe that these five main drivers are:

1. Try hard.

2. Be perfect.

3. Hurry up.

4. Please me.

5. Be strong.

These drivers are ranked in different orders, according to the selections made by the youngster in striving to please his or her parents. The child starts down the road of life practicing this central belief and doing very well, until he or she hits a stopping point, called a "stopper"!

Now comes the catch—for each one of these drivers is impossible. No one can ever do them in an entirely pleasing manner. Furthermore, as long as the person is in driver behavior, we'll see trying hard but not succeeding and enjoying; or trying to be perfect without attaining it, etc. Each time, the person necessarily hits a stopper and may then choose to return to position 1, the starting point, the driver. At least here, the individual doesn't feel bad, whereas at the stopper level, the main feeling is "I'm not OK but you and others are OK." From position 2, the person may also proceed to position 4 of Fig. 38, the final miniscript payoff. In this dismal corner, the person feels there is no hope, that nobody is OK, neither self nor others. Instead of going all the way to this dismal feeling, the person may short-cut and go to position 3, called the Vengeful Child. In this position, the Child manages to set up situations so that he or she feels OK and can look down on others, believing that they are not OK.

To summarize this triangle, the Child starts out trying to please his or her parents and be "good" by following his or her chief drivers; he or she eventually hits position 2, the stopper. Here the individual feels not OK, but believes that others are OK. He or she might stay here, might return to position 1, or might go to the Vengeful Child position where he or she feels OK but thinks others aren't. From here, the person can go back to either of the prior positions or on to position 4, the payoff, where he or she is not OK and neither is anybody else. From here, the person might choose to begin over again or to go back to any of the prior positions, or might choose some other way out, like going crazy or committing suicide or stealing a big piece of equipment and getting caught in the act.

All this may sound hopeless. It isn't. So far, we've been discussing the not-OK Miniscript. By increasing awareness of drivers and the behavior that indicates their presence, the person may be helped to change from a not-OK to OK miniscript.

OK Miniscript

As soon as you (or anyone else) becomes aware of being in your driver behavior, you may decide to go to the OK miniscript (Fig. 39). In this one, the driver is replaced with an allower; the stopper is replaced with a goer; the Vengeful Child is replaced with a be-er (or Affirming Free Child).

Let's take the instance of Jane Struggles, supervisor, who has a Try Hard driver. She frequently says things like, "It's hard for me—it's difficult for me; I've been trying. . . ." She frowns hard as she says this; she often literally strains with effort as she tries. If in the not-OK miniscript, she may go to the stopper where she realizes that she hasn't succeeded, no matter

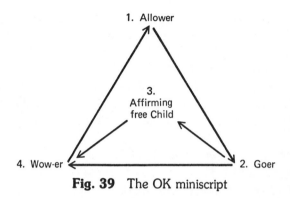

Fig. 39 The OK miniscript

how hard she has tried. She may go back to the starting point or go to the position of the Vengeful Child, where she tries so hard that others around her look lazy or even foolish and she feels virtuous and contemptuous of others. She might also go to the payoff position, where she realizes that all her efforts are fruitless because she's no good, but the job is so difficult that no one else is any good either.

If she tunes in to her driver behavior—for example, her over-use of the words indicating she's trying hard or her frown as she leans forward in her trying—she can decide to go to the OK miniscript and, instead of the driver of Try Hard, listen to the allower of "It's OK to do it. You don't have to just keep trying." If she becomes aware of the driver only when she already feels bad, at the stopper position, she can change over to a goer, such as, "It's OK to succeed." If she becomes aware only after she has gone to either position 3 or 4, she may need to ask, "What driver did I go through to get down to these feelings?" If it was a Try Hard driver, she goes back to position 1 and changes from driver to allower.

You, as a manager, may be able to help such a person right on the job. If she goes into her Try Hard driver, frowning, straining hard, telling you how hard she's been trying, and if Try Hard is your predominant driver, you may find that you soon join her in Try Hard. This is your clue to switch to your allower. As soon as you feel like you're trying unusually hard, are actually straining, that you are frowning tightly and that both of you are talking about how hard or difficult it is, then switch to the allower which is, "It's OK to *do* it. You don't have to *try* so hard." This simple awareness of moving from the Try Hard to the allower position is enough to at least help you relax, get out of your own Try Hard and *invite* others out of theirs. We say invite, because when one person goes into driver behavior he or she can't *make* the other person go into drivers. It's a very strong invitation, however.

How do you recognize the other drivers so you can shift out of them into allowers? The Hurry Up is easiest to spot because the individual is in such a hurry and shows it by pressure of speech and body movements, such as looking often at the clock, drumming fingers on the table, looking about in many different directions—almost as if looking for the fire escape. The only fire, however, is in the person with the Hurry Up driver. Fast is never fast enough for them.

Be Strong is almost the opposite. These people seldom show feelings. They hold their faces and bodies rigidly and their personalities almost equally rigidly.

Please Me is particularly easy to spot, providing you remember how children learn to please. They are small so they must look up to see if the important person is smiling. If they don't see this person smiling, they will look sideways for someone else's approval. They frequently nod their head in the "yes" series of movements. This is often so remarkable that we find ourselves pleasing *them* by nodding with them, repeating their nods until we notice that we, too, are looking up because we have nodded so much that our chins are now tucked almost onto our chests.

A Case in Point

We'll show you how drivers work. Sam, the supervisor, has been an almost perfect supervisor. He reads, studies his job, and is a very efficient, proper, punctual person. Yesterday he was different. He took twenty minutes for a coffee break instead of the regulation fifteen minutes. Today he receives this memo addressed to all supervisors: "Supervisors have been allowing their personnel to violate the regulation coffee break by exceeding fifteen minutes. Effective immediately, all supervisors will see that they and their personnel adhere rigidly to the regulation fifteen-minute breaks."

By referring back to Fig. 38, you will know that this will activate his Be Perfect driver, position 1. He then goes to position 2 and feels bad. He's been caught, he believes, doing something less than perfect. He feels discouraged that he isn't perfect. Rather than tolerate this bad feeling, he goes to position 3. He feels that he has always been good, almost perfect, and his employers have been bad with their nonsensical regulations. After all, he is the most conscientious of all supervisors there. He now decides, "I'll show them. I know how to run this department better than they do. I'll stick rigidly to their regulations and show them how silly they are." After passing on the memo to his personnel, he watches sharply. He catches Tom exceeding the regulation fifteen minutes and bawls him out. Tom replies, "That's one of the troubles with this place. Work, work, work! Nobody ever cares how you feel. I was just thinking of going home instead of working but had decided to work the day out. I'm coming down with the flu and if that's all the appreciation I get around here, I'm checking out—sick—now." Now, Sam feels that Tom is no good, the company is no good, and Sam's no good—and ends in position 4 with a final payoff of bad feelings.

What could he have done differently? After reading the memo and feeling guilty, he could have recognized that this was only another episode of his Be Perfect. Knowing this, he could have given himself the allower, "You don't have to be perfect. You're an excellent supervisor. You goofed yesterday. Feeling bad won't help. Do your usual good job." Look at the misery he would have saved for himself and his organization.

In summary, when you recognize that you are in one of your own drivers, stop your own driver behavior. This is a strong invitation to the other person to stop his or her driver behavior also. If this succeeds, you will not spend so much energy on the job, and you will almost certainly find that your efficiency and pleasure on the job actually increase.

SUGGESTED ACTIVITIES

1. Approximately what percent of your time do you spend in the following combinations of feelings?

   I'm OK—You're OK ___%
   I'm OK—You're Not OK ___%
   I'm Not OK—You're OK ___%
   I'm Not OK—You're Not OK ___%

2. In the last three weeks, you have noticed the decreased work output of a thirty-five-year-old woman in your depart-

ment. You notice that she moves more slowly than usual. Her speech is also slower than usual. She looks depressed. You tell her that you have noticed that she doesn't seem to be her usual self. She apologizes for this and says she will try harder. She still seems depressed. You want to cheer her up by telling her that things will soon be all right again. Is this a wise move? (After you have answered, read page 141 again).

3. a) What driver behavior do you show most often? Next most often? Which do you show least? (You may need to review the list on page 143). Discuss this list with a trusted friend, and have the friend rank your drivers.

   b) If you are often in the stopper position (I'm Not OK—You Are OK) or the Vengeful Child position (I'm OK—You're Not OK), ask yourself which of the five drivers you went through to get there. What allower would replace that driver? Give yourself that allower. Then follow it up with behavior appropriate to the allower. Do you notice a difference in the way you feel? In the way you work?

4. If you have not already done so, will you now consider how you would like to change. Refer to your actual and ideal egograms in item 6 of the Chapter 2 "Suggested Activities" in planning your contract.

Contracts
for Change

By this time, we trust that you have learned much about TA. It is the simplest way we know to understand and modify human behavior. Now we hope you will go one step further. We hope that you will make your own contract for change and that you will keep the contract. Such contracts have much in common with plans for change made in Managing by Objectives.

TA is similar to M.B.O. in that the concerned parties participate in making the contract for change and in having objective data by which to evaluate change. TA differs from M.B.O. in recognizing that:

- the contract must be made by the Adult ego state.

- the individual contracting for a change in the way he or she lives will also need to find new ways to get strokes as he or she changes repetitive behavior.

- the individual may defeat his or her efforts to change by playing games or by spending most of the time in pastiming when his or her goal might be increased work efficiency.

- each of us has some self-defeating tendencies in our life script.

- these tendencies operate outside of the awareness of our Adult ego states.

- we can monitor our behavior on a second-to-second basis and greatly increase the amount of time we spend in OK-ness.

Committing yourself to change and then following through on such change is one of the most-efficient ways of seeing how you can make TA work. For that reason, we now ask you to make a contract with yourself. Further, we ask that you write it, not merely read about it. We are indebted to Dr. Muriel James for much of the following material on contracts to which we have made some modifications of our own.

1. a) How do you want to be working one year from now? Where? With whom? Under what circumstances?

   b) How do you want nonwork aspects of your life to be different one year from now?

2. What behavior will *you* have to change in order to reach these goals?

3. a) As you make these changes, how will you be seen differently at work by those who know you best?

   b) How will you be seen differently away from work by those who know you best?

4. How will you prevent yourself from reaching your goals? Not write them down at all? Write them down and file them? Procrastinate? Give up in discouragement when you find changing is difficult at times? Try to get others to change so you don't need to change your own behavior?

5. When will you start changing?

6. What changes will you have completed by three months? Six months? One year?

You can change the way you feel and behave, both on the job and away from it. We are convinced that making and keeping such change contracts is one of the best ways to learn TA. We hope that you will use this method to demonstrate to yourself what you have learned from reading this book.

References

The books of Eric Berne, M.D., listed first below, constitute the backbone of transactional analysis. Almost all of these are in paperback.

1. *Games People Play*. New York: Grove Press, 1964.
2. *Principles of Group Treatment*. New York: Grove Press, 1969.
3. *Structure and Dynamics of Organizations and Groups*. New York: Grove Press, 1966.
4. *Transactional Analysis in Psychotherapy*. New York: Grove Press, 1961.
5. *Sex in Human Loving*. New York: Grove Press, 1970.
6. *What Do You Say After You Say Hello?* New York: Grove Press, 1972.

The following are simplifications or elaborations of TA concepts.

7. Harris, Thomas A., M.D. *I'm OK—You're OK*. New York: Harper & Row, 1967.

8. James, Muriel, Ph.D., and Dorothy Jongeward, M. Ed. *Born to Win*. Reading, Mass.: Addison-Wesley, 1971.

9. James, Muriel, Ph.D., and Dorothy Jongeward, M.Ed. *Winning With People*. Reading, Mass.: Addison-Wesley, 1971.

10. Jongeward, Dorothy, M.Ed., and Dru Scott. *Affirmative Action for Women*. Reading, Mass.: Addison-Wesley, 1973.

11. Jongeward, Dorothy, M.Ed. *Everybody Wins; Transactional Analysis Applied to Organizations*. Reading, Mass.: Addison-Wesley, 1973.

12. Meininger, Jut. *Success through Transactional Analysis*. New York: Grosset & Dunlap, 1973.

13. Steiner, Claude. *Scripts People Live*. New York: Bantam, 1975.